FAMILY MATH
for
Young Children:
Comparing

FAMILY MATH

for
Young Children:
Comparing

Grace Dávila Coates
Jean Kerr Stenmark

Illustrated by Rose Craig
Cover Art by Ann Humphrey Williams

The Lawrence Hall of Science is a public science center, teacher inservice institution, and research unit in science and mathematics education at the University of California, Berkeley. For many years, it has developed curricula and teaching strategies to improve mathematics, science, and computer education at all levels, and to increase public understanding of those areas.

For information about the FAMILY MATH program or additional copies of the book, contact:

FAMILY MATH
Lawrence Hall of Science
University of California
Berkeley, CA 94720-5200

(510) 642-1823 - program
(510) 642-1910 or (800) 897-5036 - books
(510) 643-5757 FAX

Credits:

Editor: BRIAN GOTHBERG

Cover Illustrator: ANN WILLIAMS

Interior Illustrator: ROSE CRAIG

Photography: ELIZABETH CREWS

Publishing Assistant: DEBORAH FIERRO MARTÍNEZ

Printer: U.C. PRINTING SERVICES

ISBN 0-912511-27-3

Table of Contents

A MATHEMATICAL ENVIRONMENT   15
    Mathematics In Your Home   16
    Everyday Estimation   20
    Questions That Promote Mathematical Thinking   22
    Acknowledging Your Child's Work   24

INVESTIGATIONS, ACTIVITIES, AND EXPLORATIONS   27
    The Activity Pages Include: 28
    Organizing Information   30
    Nuts and Bolts   37
    Now I Am Tall   38
    Inside, Outside, On   40
    Copy-Cats   42
    Papel Picado   44
    Rag Bag   46
    Share a Square Mobile   50
    Create A Puzzle Jr.   52
    Direction   54
    Button Boxes   62
    Button, Button, Where Is The Button?   66
    Measuring Spoons   68
    Paper Plate Math   70
    Tracing Shapes   73
    Mixtures — Bean Salads and Fish Bowls   74
    I'm a Shape   84
    Moon and Stars   88
    Same Yet Different   90
    Many Shapes   92
    Love Notes Quilt Patch   94
    Name That Shape   97
    Patterns All Around   98
    Make-a-Pair   100
    Make-a-Pair Cards   103
    Looking at Letters   105
    Tell Me What You See   114
    What's Alike About You and Me?   116
    Me and My Toys   118
    This is In and This is Not   120
    What Is Missing?   124
    My Rule, Your Rule   126
    Make a Game   128
    Making Spinners   132
    Shadows   135
    In a Secret Treasure Box   138

Table of Contents (continued)

COLLECTIONS AND TREASURES   139
    Collections   140
    Stamps Galore!   142
    Leaf Treasures   144
    Seashells   146
    Rocks   148

HOW'S MY CHILD DOING?   151

SHARING FAMILY MATH FOR YOUNG CHILDREN   159
    Sharing FAMILY MATH   160
    Class Evaluation   161
    Planning Check-Sheet   163
    FAMILY MATH for Young Children   164
    FAMILY MATH Class Notes   165
    Sample Schedule   169
    Sample Planning Sheet   173
    Interest Centers and Samples   174
    Interest Center Examples   175

MORE RESOURCES   181
    Mathematics Generally Covered   182
    Resources   192
    Bibliography   193

INDEX   194

Preface

We are delighted to present the first volume of the much-requested FAMILY MATH books for families with young children, from about four years old to eight years old. We hope to be able to publish at least two or three more books to complete the series.

FAMILY MATH is one of the EQUALS programs at the Lawrence Hall of Science, University of California at Berkeley. Since 1977, the EQUALS programs have helped elementary and secondary educators and families acquire methods and materials to make mathematics more accessible for all students, with a special focus on those from groups that are not well-represented in mathematics: students of color, girls, children from low-income families, and those from language minority groups.

EQUALS and FAMILY MATH programs support a problem-solving approach to mathematics, including having students and families working together in groups, using active learning methods, and incorporating a broad mathematics curriculum presented in a variety of contexts.

In FAMILY MATH, special focus is on children and adult family members working and enjoying mathematics together and sharing their thinking about problems. Both children and adults contribute to the process as they learn from each other.

We find that the families of FAMILY MATH are better able to participate in the life of their children's schools. They become more aware of the role mathematics plays in education, and feel more confident in helping their children with math. Often, they become leaders of FAMILY MATH classes themselves.

We hope you and your family will enjoy this book.

Grace Dávila Coates
Jean Kerr Stenmark

Acknowledgements

We deeply appreciate the continued ideas, support, and counsel of present and past colleagues from the EQUALS Program and the Lawrence Hall of Science at the University of California, Berkeley: Terri Belcher, José Franco (Director, EQUALS), Kay Gilliland, Nancy Kreinberg (Founding Director, EQUALS), Karen Mayfield-Ingram, Virginia Thompson (Director, FAMILY MATH), Bob Whitlow, Kathryn Baston, Bob Capune, Carol Gray, Ellen Humm, Louise Lang, Gen Llamas, Deborah Martínez, Linda Morgan, Helen Raymond, Angélica López, Hilda Perez, Patricia Zuno, and Miguel Casillas.

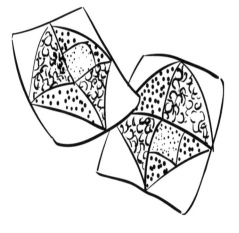

Special thanks to Brian Gothberg for generously donating his time to the editing and design of this book. We are also deeply grateful to Ann Williams, who translated our work into a beautiful cover and donated it to this project.

Some of the activities were originally created by people outside our program. The sources have been acknowledged where known, and all of the activities have been substantially modified.

And most of all, we thank the teachers, parents, and children who have been part of the exciting development of FAMILY MATH for Young Children.

I Remember When I Was Young...

Do you remember mathematical kinds of things you did when you were young?

Write down or make tapes of stories of some of your memories.

This is for both grownups and children. Everybody has something to remember.

Make your stories into a booklet or collection of tapes, so they can be shared with others. Gather together some of your friends, family, or neighbors for a FAMILY MATH class and have a sharing session.

You might think about games you played, or trips to the grocery store or other shops, or chores you did, or trips you made, or folk tales you were told. Use your imagination!

Here's a story told to us by Esteban (Steve) Zapiain:

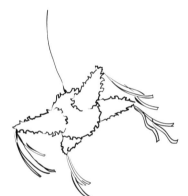

I remember fiestas!

At Baptisms (Bautizos) the sponsor (padrino) would throw a handful of coins up in the air for all the little kids (la chiquillada) to gather up. As I got older, I soon realized that silver coins had more value than copper. Later, I discovered that the difference between small coins (dimes) and larger coins (pennies) depended on the denomination.

However, at all ages, the more coins you could gather, the better!

Piñatas were and still are exciting. To make the game a little more fair, younger children of two, three, or four, were not blindfolded. From the age of five or six (school age), you were turned around once for each year of your age. As kids got older or bigger, they would be "tricked" by the adults. In these cases, the adults would pretend to lose count and would begin again. And so the oldest were most dizzy, while the youngest learned to count.

What is FAMILY MATH?

It's parents and kids enjoying and learning math together.

It's doing activities and playing games.

It's using beans, buttons, pennies, and toys to solve math problems.

It's being friendly with numbers and shapes.

It's exploring shapes and geometry.

It's working and talking with others.

It's estimating with numbers and sizes.

It's learning how math connects with real life.

A Mathematical Environment

Mathematics In Your Home

As families and educators, most of us know that reading aloud to our children on a regular basis provides a strong foundation for success and enjoyment in reading.

But when it comes to mathematics, many of us don't know where to start. Do we buy flash cards to teach them the basic facts? Do we make them memorize rules? How do you feel now when your children ask you for help?

Do you remember your own experiences in mathematics? Was it fun or painful? Did you feel successful? In high school did you continue to take math after it was not required?

This book is for you and your child. It is about loving mathematics. It is about learning with your child, and, if you like, learning with other families.

Whether you do the activities with your child or with a group, these activities are meant to be fun. There is no pressure to rush toward right answers, or mastery of ideas. There's no test. You can take your time with an activity and move on to the next one whenever you or your children are ready.

The beauty of mathematics is in patterns. Math can be found in art, music, nature, dance, textiles, and many other everyday things and events.

DOING MATHEMATICS AT HOME

These ideas will help you create a warm and nurturing environment for mathematical explorations for your family. You will see them repeated throughout the book in different ways.

Believe that your children can succeed and let them know it. Model persistence and not giving up. We teach by what we do. Our children emulate us.

Talk with your child and really listen to what they are saying. If you do not know an answer to a problem, ask your child questions about it. You will find questions to help you do this throughout the book.

Problem-solving processes are as critical as the answers. Knowing *how* to find an answer without giving up is a lifetime skill. Getting the correct answer to a problem is not as important as the behaviors surrounding it.

Practice being a keen observer with your children whenever possible. Notice patterns on fabrics, details in plants, clouds, trees, and tiles.

Encourage your child to exchange ideas with their peers. This becomes even more important as your child grows older.

Provide a special place for study. Let your child help determine where that place will be. Making choices is part of becoming a good problem solver.

Establish positive homework habits. A consistent schedule helps children know what is expected, and they can plan around it. There is a high correlation between success in math and the amount of homework done.

Do not expect that all homework will be easy, but always support your child. Look for questions you can ask that will point in the right direction.

Ask your child's teacher about a plan for your child. Talk about the teacher's plans for her mathematics program.

Make time to visit your child's classroom and participate in school events. Children whose parents are involved in schools experience more success than those whose parents never visit the school.

Be aware of what tests your child will be taking. Ask about the implications for your child. Know that some tests will not measure your child's true abilities, capacities, or attributes. They may not measure divergent thinking, persistence, or having effective strategies.

Resist drilling your child on math content. Do not use math homework as punishment or reward. Learning happens best when there is intrinsic motivation for wanting to understand something.

Model persistence and pleasure with mathematics. Make games of counting. Talk about patterns you see in the world; describe details of things you see. Try to integrate mathematics into your family's time together.

Above all enjoy mathematics, your child, and yourself!

Everyday Estimation

Kids love to guess about numbers. They also want to be exactly correct. You can provide your child with many opportunities to practice this important math skill.

You can practice at the grocery store, when weighing fruits or vegetables. You can practice on the way home from school by guessing how many steps you take to cross the street, or how many minutes it takes you to drive to school.

Toys, beans, pebbles, macaroni, or other items can be used for estimating. You may need containers like jars, small plastic bags, or any see-through container you may have around the house.

Here are some possibilities:

Δ   A small jar filled with about ten large marshmallows (don't squeeze them). You can also fill a same-size jar with smaller marshmallows and compare the different amounts. You can ask younger children to compare the two jars and tell you something that is true about the jars' contents.

Δ   A plastic bag with string in it. Is the string as long as your child is tall? As you are tall?

Δ   A jar filled with large pasta (like shell macaroni) and a same-size jar filled with small pasta.

Δ   A large jar filled with tennis balls (up to about ten for younger children).

Δ   100 kernels of popcorn (unpopped) and then the same popped.

Δ   Estimate the number of jelly beans in a bag before you eat any of them.

Δ   Can you think of other things to estimate?

Estimation Questions:

Δ   Write your names. How many beans do you think it will take to cover the letters?

Δ   Which name took up the most beans? Are there any other names you would like to try?

Δ   How many basketballs would it take to fill your car?

Δ   How many minutes will it take to get to school or to the market from your house?

Δ   What other things can you estimate?

Creating these opportunities will improve your child's estimating skills and accuracy.

Questions That Promote Mathematical Thinking

Many parents report that it is difficult to know what questions to ask, because they do not have much experience in mathematics.

The questions on the following page were developed by educators and parents who have gone through FAMILY MATH for Young Children workshops or classes. We asked them to think of types of questions they might ask that did not have a "yes" or "no" answer, or only one possible answer, like, "What is two plus one?"

As you ask these questions, listen carefully to your child's responses. Be directly involved in the moment, and be careful not to take over the work or the process.

Be sensitive to when your child is ready to move about or go on to something else.

These questions will help you keep the conversation and learning going as you explore mathematics with your child. They promote thinking and further learning. You may want to add some questions of your own.

Δ   What do you suppose would happen if...?

Δ   What will you do next?

Δ   I wonder...?

Δ   How can we check to see how close your guess is?

Δ   Why do you think that?

Δ   How did you figure that out?

Δ   Do you have any ideas about how we might begin?

Δ   How can we do this differently?

Δ   Hmm-mm, I had not thought of that. Tell me more about it.

Δ   What other ways can we show that?

Δ   Tell me about your design.

Δ   How did you decide which objects go in the circle?

Δ   What other things can we find shaped like a square/circle/triangle...?

Δ   What would you do with this?

Δ   Tell me how you did that.

WHOA! Don't ask these questions all at once. One or two well-placed questions go a long way toward encouraging thinking and creating deeper understanding.

Acknowledging Your Child's Work

Let your child know that you are aware of the thoughtful work, the creative ideas, or interesting choices that have been made.

Comment on the work by making observations.

♡ "I see that you have lined up three triangles and two circles. Tell me about your pattern."

♡ "Let's share your pattern with Mom/Dad after dinner."

♡ "I think your solution is interesting. Let's share it with…"

♡ "That is a creative way of thinking about it. Let me know what you decide."

♡ "That is an interesting plan. Is there anything you want me to do?"

♡ "You changed the rules? Tell me what they are so I can play the game with you."

♡ "Thank you for setting the table. I see you placed a napkin on each dish."

♡ "Thank you for putting your socks away. I noticed you matched a yellow sock with a blue sock. Can you tell me why you decided to do that?"

Acknowledge your child's work by describing it, rather than qualifying it by saying only that it is "neat", "wonderful", or "good". This is not to say you should not admire the work. Children want to please parents, but they also learn not to value feedback when it is always the same or without specificity.

Do ask your child's opinion of the work that has been done. This fosters accountability, self reflection, and autonomy.

Ask questions instead of making corrections (see the "sock-matching" statement above).

Accept unusual solutions, or solutions you had not expected.

Take a role in your child's activities without taking over.

Investigations, Activities, and Explorations

The Activity Pages Include:

All the activities in this book are about comparing. They are introductions to ideas and concepts. Each activity page is marked by the various headings described here.

THIS IS ABOUT

Under this heading, you will see a list of concepts or skills addressed in the activity, such as counting, measuring, estimating, sorting, observing, describing, and other important problem-solving skills.

YOU WILL NEED

This section lists the materials you will need. Most of the materials are items which can be easily found or collected. Children and parents have given ideas about objects in their daily lives, and things of interest. We have included models and ideas for creating your own sorting mats, graphs, number cubes, and spinners. You don't need to spend a lot of money to learn mathematics.

GETTING READY

Sometimes you will need to prepare or collect materials prior to sitting down with your child to work on a project. This section describes what you will need before you and your child begin to explore. You may want to include your child in this part of the process. Children enjoy being part of making preparations.

ACTIVITY INSTRUCTIONS

The instructions are numbered and easy to follow. You may want to change the rules, the outcomes, and even the materials. We encourage such creativity! The activities or games have been tried out with families, educators, and other community groups. Many of the wonderful extension or adaptation ideas were developed by interested persons like you.

INSIGHTS, HINTS, AND QUESTIONS

We all have diverse levels of experience with mathematics. Sometimes you will see notes at the end of the activities that give you more background information, other ways to ask questions, or hints that help clarify ideas. These have been included as a result of parents' requests for more ideas and information. We hope you will find these notes helpful.

Organizing Information

The following charts are included as suggestions for how objects might be sorted, classified, numbered, or represented. If you or your child wish to use them, copy the designs onto other paper or make photo-copies so that you can use them for many activities.

The best thing you can do for your child is to ask how the work or information might be organized. When your child finds a different way to make a set, investigate a pattern, or assign items to particular groups, ask questions about the thinking that went into the decision.

Provide alternative materials such as yarn or string for making circles or other shapes. Recycled margarine tubs, frozen food trays, and aluminum pie tins, are just a few examples of containers you can use for many of the activities in this book.

RESIST the urge to make your child do things the way you might do them. You can create a pattern, or a set, and ask your child to guess your rule. As you keep the conversation and the exploration going, your child will create other possible solutions and come to a new understanding as different strategies unfold.

How did you figure out in which group the ring would go?

It goes with all the small things.

I see, what about that small key with the pennies?

It's with all the metal things, the other stuff is not made of metal.

INSIGHT

Organizing information helps us keep track of what has been done. Children who develop this skill will have greater success in mathematics and science. Both subjects require us to keep records, illustrate, and explain our work to others.

Venn Diagram

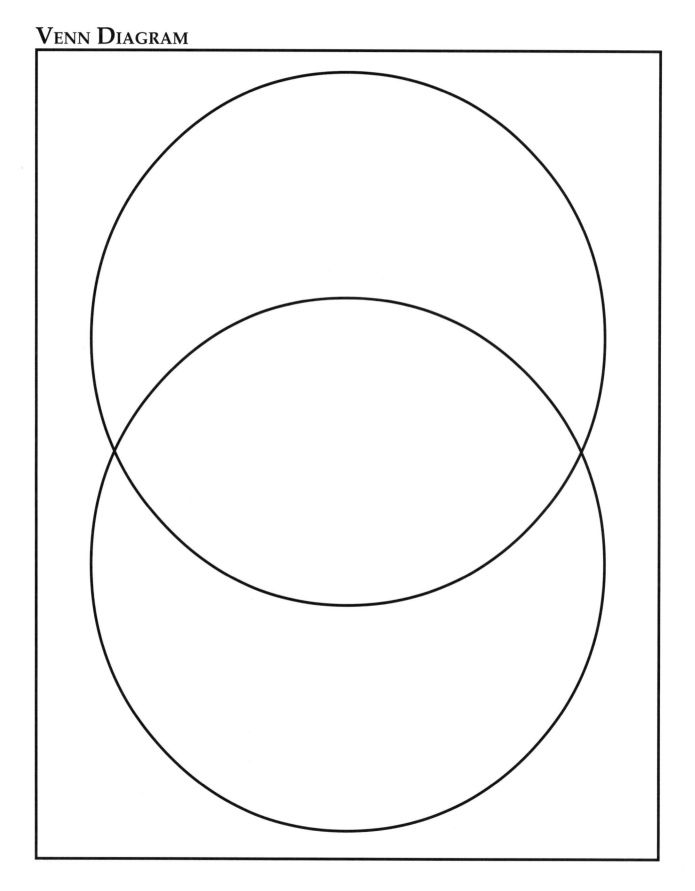

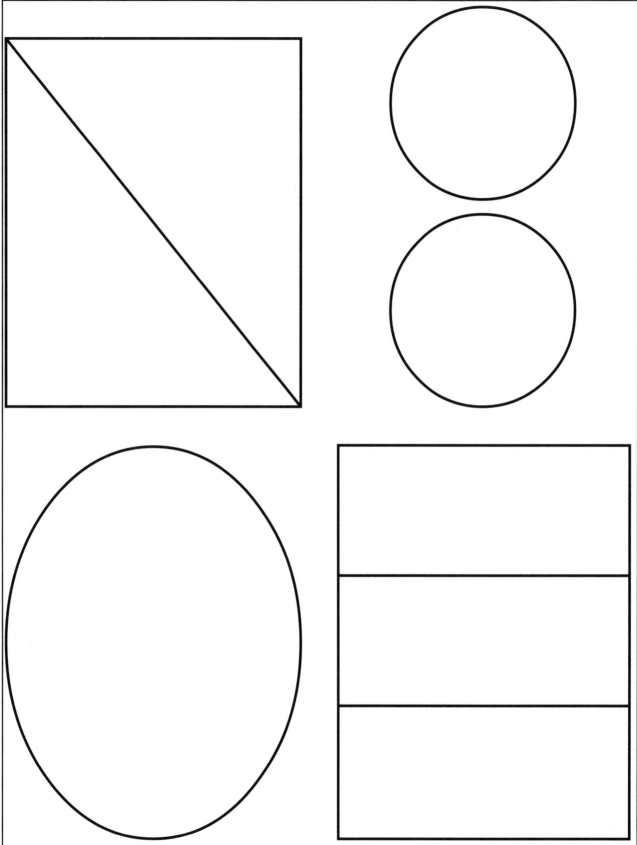

BAR CHART

FAMILY MATH for Young Children

HUNDRED CHART

1	2	3	4	5	6	7	8	9	10
11	12	13	14	15	16	17	18	19	20
21	22	23	24	25	26	27	28	29	30
31	32	33	34	35	36	37	38	39	40
41	42	43	44	45	46	47	48	49	50
51	52	53	54	55	56	57	58	59	60
61	62	63	64	65	66	67	68	69	70
71	72	73	74	75	76	77	78	79	80
81	82	83	84	85	86	87	88	89	90
91	92	93	94	95	96	97	98	99	**100**

TWENTY-FIVE CHART

1	2	3	4	5
6	7	8	9	10
11	12	13	14	15
16	17	18	19	20
21	22	23	24	25

Nuts and Bolts

THIS IS ABOUT

Δ   counting

Δ   visual reasoning

Δ   matching one to one

YOU WILL NEED

Δ   nuts and bolts of different sizes, in pairs that fit each other

Δ   some beans

ACTIVITY

1.   Empty the bag of nuts and bolts onto the table. Start with about five pairs.

2.   Ask your child to choose a nut.

3.   You pick a bolt that might fit it. If they fit, you get a score of 1 (or put one bean in your bowl) because you got it on the first try.

   If they don't fit, choose another bolt and try it. If it fits, you get a score of 2 because you got it on the second try, and so forth.

4.   Take turns until you have paired up all the nuts and bolts, and add up your score (beans). Keeping score is optional.

5.   Try the game again and compare your first score with the second one. The object is to match the nuts and bolts with the least amount of tries.

   This is not a competitive game. The score you keep is for keeping record of your progress as a team.

INSIGHT

After you have tried this for awhile, your child will get better at matching the correct sizes. This is important in developing your child's ability in visual estimation and accuracy.

Now I Am Tall

THIS IS ABOUT

Δ   comparing

Δ   sizes

Δ   shapes

YOU WILL NEED

Δ   ourselves

GETTING READY

Find an indoor or outdoor space where you will be able to move freely.

Can't keep my kids sitting still too long! I've read that they need "large muscle" activities. What does that mean?

Must be like jumping and stretching and running and hopping. Mine like really BIG things to do.

What kind of things would be "not large muscle" activities?

Oh, I guess things like writing, and picking up little things, and sewing, and — well, probably TV doesn't use large muscles, either! And moving helps with ideas like short, wide, tall, straight, round, and lots of other things.

ACTIVITY

Stand facing each other or side by side. Say (or sing) these comparing words, and act them out.

"Now I'm short."

"Now I'm tall."

"Now I'm wide."

"Now I'm narrow."

"Now I'm round."

"Now I'm square."

"Now my arms are sloped."

"Now they're flat."

"Now I'm straight."

"Now I'm bent."

"Now I'm standing."

"Now I'm hopping."

Make up your own comparing words.

"If I were a tree, I would be…"

INSIGHT

Young children should not be required to sit still for long. They need to be able to move around. It's a good idea now and then to stop "work" and do this or some other activity that lets them move all their muscles.

Inside, Outside, On

THIS IS ABOUT

△ experience with shapes

△ being inside, outside, or on a shape

YOU WILL NEED

△ chalk, or a long string

GETTING READY

This is a game for two or more people.

Draw a large circle on the sidewalk or playground, or make a circle shape with string or yarn.

We're learning about shapes and positions by moving back and forth on a circle.

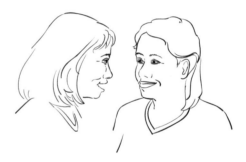

Why can't we just tell them what the words mean?

There's an old saying that starts out "I hear and I forget." and ends with "I do and I understand."

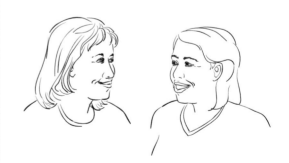

Oh, you mean they remember better if they act it out? That makes sense.

ACTIVITY

1. Have everybody stand just outside the circle.

2. Take turns giving directions, going around the circle (either clockwise or counter-clockwise—your choice!).

3. When a direction is given, everybody does what is said. For example:

> two hops INSIDE the circle
> three jumps OUTSIDE the circle
> four slides to the left ON the circle

4. Think of other actions of your own, too, such as bending down, squatting, walking, clapping, or snapping fingers.

5. You might even try making up a chant. For example:

My name is Daniel.
Stand ON the line
and slide 4 times to the Right!

My name is Tania.
I like to jump!
Jump 3 times OUTSIDE.

Copy-Cats

THIS IS ABOUT

Δ   symmetry

Δ   spatial reasoning

Δ   using scissors

YOU WILL NEED

Δ   some blank sheets of paper or the grid paper

Δ   paste, scissors

Δ   some cut-out shapes in different colors or designs, beans, or small macaroni

GETTING READY

Fold your paper in half. Each partner chooses a side that will be their space.

Share the shapes or items between the two partners so that each person has an identical set of items. For example, each person should have the same kind and number of red triangles, pinto beans, elbow macaroni, and so on.

ACTIVITY

1.   Have your child place a shape anywhere on her side of the paper. You copy by placing an identical shape (and color) on your side.

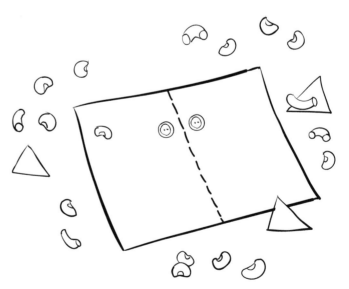

2. Continue taking turns and copying until you've taken five turns each, or until you think you have enough things on your page.

3. Once you think that your sides "match," paste or glue the objects to the paper.

4. How closely did your partner copy your design? How can you find out?

5. Try it again. This time you go first.

Can you and your child think of some things that already look the same on both sides? This is called "symmetry."

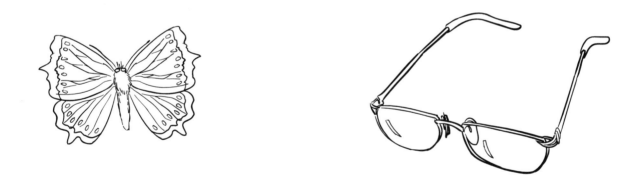

INSIGHT

Be the copy-cat first. This way, you provide a model for your child. Let your child choose which work should be displayed. Ask questions about why that particular piece was chosen. This is the beginning of children looking at their own work and learning to make decisions about what they like or do not like about it.

Papel Picado

THIS IS ABOUT

Δ symmetry

Δ using scissors

Δ folding paper

YOU WILL NEED

Δ scissors

Δ clear tape

Δ string

Δ tissue paper (the kind that is used for gift-wrapping), recycled gift wrap or wax paper

ACTIVITY

1. Cut a sheet of tissue paper into a rectangle about eight inches by eleven inches, or if you like, it can be a smaller rectangle.

2. Fold in half (in any direction).

3. Fold it in half again (in any direction).

4. Fold it in half one more time.

5. Try cutting tiny triangles at intervals along one side, like this:

6. Make some more cuts. Experiment by cutting out other shapes like half circles, or half diamonds. Try combining different shapes.

7. Unfold the paper and see what wonderful designs you have created! Tape your papel picado on some string and hang it up.

In many Latino communities papel picado is used as decoration for birthday parties, *tardeadas* (afternoon get-togethers) and other special events.

Some papel picado has cut-out shapes: birds, suns, moons, and stars.

How can you find out if your papel picado is symmetrical?

INSIGHT

Younger children (four and five year-olds) may cut paper without folding it. They may begin by cutting short random pieces as they learn to control the scissors. In this case, start a collection of cut-ups. Revisit it when your child is in first or second grade. Children like to compare their present work to their "when I was a little kid" work.

Rag Bag

THIS IS ABOUT

Δ   using language in mathematics

Δ   size and texture

Δ   describing and comparing

YOU WILL NEED

Δ   pieces of cardboard in various sizes, from small (1" by 1") to medium (up to 3" by 5")

Δ   scraps of fabric or other textured materials, such as velvet, satin, cotton, denim, sandpaper, linoleum, foil, burlap, wallpaper, and so on.

Δ   glue

Δ   scissors

Δ   a paper bag or shoebox

Language is really important in mathematics, isn't it? We're all learning to explain our thinking.

And language helps us organize our thinking and communicate about it, just like people in most jobs.

GETTING READY

1. Let the children help.

2. Cut pieces of fabric or other materials to fit the cardboard pieces.

3. Glue the cut pieces onto the cardboard pieces, and let them dry.

4. If you can, make small and large pieces from the same fabric, such as a small and a large burlap, a small and a large velvet, and so on.

5. Put some of the completed cards into a paper bag or shoebox, ready for the activities.

After you have created the squares take time to observe the differences and similarities of the colors, textures, shapes, or other characteristics.

On the following pages you will find variations of Rag Bag.

Sometimes we might need to get started by asking each other questions like these:

What can you tell me about the size?

How does it feel to touch it?

What do you see about the shape?

What about the color?

ACTIVITY 1: TELL IT LIKE IT IS

1. Put four or five different cards into the bag or box. Shake (gently!). Reach in (no peeking) and pull out one of the cards, then describe it.

2. Tell everything you notice.

3. Continue with the other cards in the bag, one at a time.

ACTIVITY 2: TWO-CARD DIFFERENCES

1. Set out two cards.

2. Together, look at the cards and describe as many differences as you can.

3. Think about size, color, shape, texture (such as fuzzy or smooth), temperature (warm or cold), or even what the material was used for.

4. Try the same with other pairs of cards.

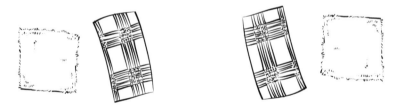

ACTIVITY 3: MATCH-UP

1. Put two or three pairs of cards that match in texture or size into the bag. Reach into the bag and pull out one of the cards. Then reach in and feel around to see if you can pull out the matching card.

2. Keep trying until you have a match.

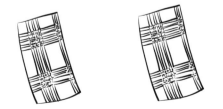

ACTIVITY 4: DIFFERENCES

1. Put about five or six cards into the bag.

2. Have one person reach in and pull out a card, then the other person.

3. Put the two cards together and tell how they are alike and how they are different.

ACTIVITY 5: A STORY

1. Take out your favorite card and tell a story about it.

2. Take out two or three cards and tell a story about their adventures.

" and then the little yellow triangle found his friend at the park..."

ACTIVITY 6: AN ORDERLY ROW

1. Arrange several of the cards in an orderly row, such as from smoothest to roughest, or from thickest to thinnest, or from darkest to lightest.

2. Make up challenges of your own.

Share a Square Mobile

THIS IS ABOUT

△ geometry

△ language

YOU WILL NEED

△ a straw or dowel (eight to ten inches long)

△ thin string or yarn

△ crayons or markers for coloring the squares

△ five or seven square pieces of construction paper, about four inches by four inches

ACTIVITY

1. Take a square and fold it in half, then cut on the folded line. Give one half to your partner.

2. The second person takes a square and folds it in half in a different way and gives the other half to the other person.

3. Working together, try to figure out what other shapes you can make from the remaining squares. Make two of each so that at the end you both have the same number of shapes.

What shapes did you create?

How many shapes do each of you have?

If you do not have construction paper handy, use the cardboard from cereal boxes, and cover it with recycled gift wrap or scraps of fabric.

4. Measure a piece of string that is three times as long as your straw and pull the string through the straw, and tie a knot in the string. (See sample below.)

5. Attach the shapes to different-size pieces of string and tie them on the straw so they hang in different lengths. Hang the mobile in your child's favorite spot.

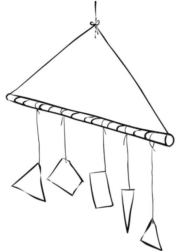

JUST FOR FUN

Write words on the shapes that tell how you feel when you are with each other, or tell the things you enjoy doing together.

INSIGHT

Having children trace, fold, and cutout their own shapes helps their understanding of the attributes or characteristics of the different shapes. It also helps them develop their small (fine) muscle coordination.

Create A Puzzle Jr.

THIS IS ABOUT

Δ   geometry

Δ   looking at different shapes

Δ   solving puzzles

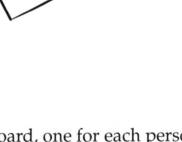

YOU WILL NEED

Δ   scissors

Δ   cardboard (cereal boxes are great)

Δ   old calendars or magazines

Δ   glue or paste

ACTIVITY

1.   Cut two six-inch squares from a piece of cardboard, one for each person. If you are using a cereal box, your cardboard squares already have a picture on them; skip steps two and three.

2.   Cut two six-inch square pictures from a magazine or old calendar. Make sure the pictures are the same size as the cardboard square.

3.   Paste the picture to each square, and let them dry for a few minutes.

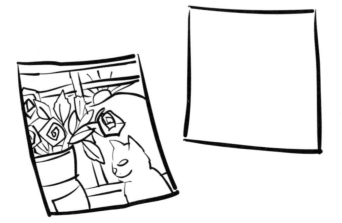

4. Make one straight cut in any direction. For example:

5. Make a second cut:

Fit the three pieces together to make sure you can solve the puzzle.

6. Make a third cut, scramble the pieces, and try putting your puzzle together.

7. Exchange your puzzle with a partner.

For a more challenging puzzle, flip it over to the side with no picture on it.

Note:

Try cutting out two squares from the same calendar picture. This way when you put your puzzle together with your child's, they form a connected picture.

INSIGHT

Exploring the attributes of different shapes by building and solving a puzzle helps children develop their spatial visual skills.

Direction

THIS ACTIVITY IS ABOUT

Δ   direction and directionality,
    such as up or down, left or right,
    front or back, and so on

YOU WILL NEED

Δ   three or four blocks

Δ   crayons

Δ   squares of paper, other markers
    of different colors like red, blue,
    yellow, or green

Δ   space maps like the ones below

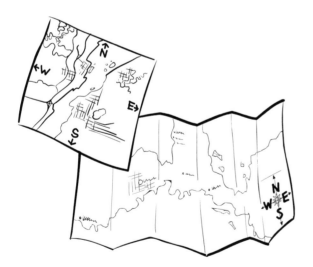

*Sometimes when I say something to
my child, like up or down, she doesn't
seem to understand, especially when
we're talking about a piece of paper on
the table.*

*Yes, what's the bottom of the paper: the
part touching the table, or the part
closest to us?*

*Mm–hmm. We need a logical way of
deciding on exact meanings for certain
words.*

GETTING READY

Directions and directionality can be confusing for all of us. It's important to stop and think about the language we use.

Often there's not a single right way of interpreting the directions. Sometimes it's just a meaning we agree on.

For example, talk about:

◊ rows, which go across, and columns, which go up and down

◊ back yards and front yards

◊ the back of the drawer

◊ the top of the table, and the top of the paper on the table

◊ and other real-life ideas about direction.

I have an idea — let's make up some "space maps" that we can use to solve the problems, like these:

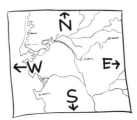

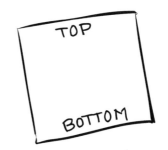

We might even try some maps without square corners:

ACTIVITY 1: WHICH DIRECTION?

Talk about these ideas, ONE AT A TIME, as they come up in the activities or at other times. The meaning often depends on circumstances and can be very confusing unless acted out and discussed.

The point of these is not for us to memorize, but to practice some of the various meanings. If children seem confused, stop, and try the ideas again when they are a little older.

Up and Down

Usually up means away from the earth and down means toward the earth. Even if you were lying on the grass, up would probably still mean toward the sky, rather than toward your head.

Top and Bottom

But if you say top and bottom, it's a different story. The top of your head is still the top, even if you are lying down. But the top of your body might be the part farthest from the grass!

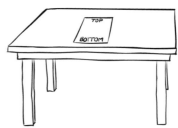

Sitting at a table, the top of the paper is usually farthest from you, and the bottom is nearest. (And the part away from the table is usually the front, while the part that touches the table is the back.)

Back and Front

The front of my shirt is still the front, whether I am wearing it or not.

If I'm at the back of the line looking forward, the front of the line is the part farthest away from me.

Sitting at a table with a piece of paper, is there a back and front of the paper?

Right and Left

If you and I are facing the same direction, "the right" means the same to both of us. But if we are sitting on opposite sides of the table, what happens when we point at each other with our right hands?

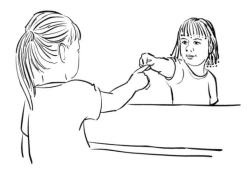

North, South, East, and West

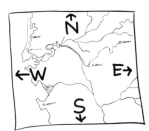

When we are facing North, East is to our right, West is to our left, and South is behind us. If we are looking at a map, we can turn the map around so that North is at the bottom, and then everything looks different! What happens when we look at the map in a mirror?

Activity 2: All in a Row

2-Block Rows

How many ways can two blocks, one red and one blue, be put together, side by side?

3-Block Rows

How many arrangements can be made with three blocks in a row, if each block is a different color? Ask each other questions. For example, you might ask:

If red is first in line, which block could be last?

What would be in the middle?

If red is first again, could another one be last this time?

What else could be first?

4-Block Rows

Try the same with four blocks. Remember: each block should be a different color. Is there a middle block?

Rows or Columns

Put out three blocks, so they go from in front of you toward the other side of the table.

Follow these directions to arrange the blocks.

> The red is closest to you.
> The yellow is closest to the red.
> Where could the blue be?

Is this a row or a column?

INSIGHT

*Making sense of where **things** are in relationship to where **we** are occurs naturally. These activities help us describe what those relationships are.*

ACTIVITY 3: COLOR LINES OF THREE

Arrange each color line with red, blue, and yellow blocks.

1. Red is in back of the blue.
    Blue is between yellow and red.
    Where is yellow?

2. Yellow is on the bottom.
    Blue is in the middle.
    Where is red?

3. Blue is to the right of yellow.
    Red is to the right of blue.
    Where is yellow?

4. Yellow is in front of blue.
    Red is behind blue.
    Where is blue?

5. Yellow is on top.
    Red is between blue and yellow.
    Where is blue?

Make up new problems of your own. How about using:

*   beside

*   right next to

*   near but not touching

*   over (or under)

ACTIVITY 4: COLOR LINES OF FOUR

Arrange each color line with red, blue, yellow, and green. Sit together on the same side of the table.

1. Blue is behind red.
   Yellow is in the very front.
   Red is between blue and green.

2. Red is right of yellow.
   Yellow is right of blue.
   Green is right of red.

3. Red is left of blue.
   Green is right of yellow.
   Blue is left of yellow.

4. Green is north of all others.
   Red is south of all others.
   Yellow is south of blue.

5. Blue is east of red.
   Green is west of red.
   Yellow is east of green.

Some problems may have more than one solution.

Make up new problems of your own.

Can you make up one that uses north, south, east, and west?

INSIGHT

Children clarify and strengthen their logic and reasoning abilities when they sort things, consider possible results, or make conclusions based on given information.

Button Boxes

THIS IS ABOUT

Δ   being friendly with numbers

Δ   practicing adding

YOU WILL NEED

Δ   buttons
    or small blocks
    or bottle-caps
    or design your own cardboard
    buttons

Δ   if you like, you might cut apart
    an egg carton to make the boxes
    shown

GETTING READY

Part of the object of this activity is to practice combining small numbers to make larger numbers in an informal way, with things we can move around.

When you have played the game a few times, make up different sets of "boxes," to practice other number combinations.

With the boxes in this activity, at least two of the suggested combinations will not be possible. What are they?

Why buttons? Why can't we just write down the numbers and have the kids add them, the way we did when we were in school?

We move buttons around and match each button to its own box, so they are part of the numbers.

When do they learn about adding numbers together?

When they find that they can combine a 2-box and a 3-box to make 5, that's adding!

FAMILY MATH for Young Children

ACTIVITY

The Story

You're helping with the button booth at the school fair. The buttons are very special. Each button must have its own space in a box. You can't sell a box with any empty spaces!

Since you can't sell a box with any empty spaces, if you put a button into one space of a box, you also must put buttons into the other spaces of that box.

Here is a practice box. How many buttons could you put into this box?

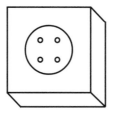

(Only one, of course!)

Here's another practice box. How many buttons would it hold?

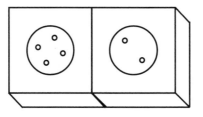

(two buttons)

If you used both of these boxes, how many buttons could you put in?

On the following pages is a set of boxes and a list of orders to fill. How many of the orders can you fill with those boxes?

Button Boxes (continued)

These are the button boxes you have for the button booth orders at the school fair. You may use as many boxes as you need for each order.

Talk together about each order.

Each button must have its own space.

You can't sell a box with any empty spaces.

On the next page are some button orders.

Box A

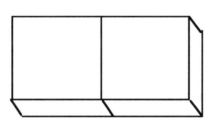

Box B

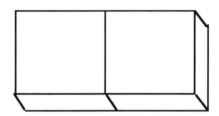

Box C

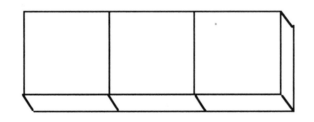

Box D

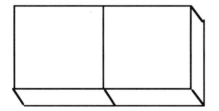

Box E

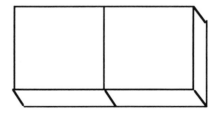

How many buttons will go in:

Box A? _____

Box B? _____

Box C? _____

Boxes A and B? _____

Boxes C and D? _____

Boxes C, D and E? _____

Make up some of your own combinations.

Here are some orders. Which boxes would you use for these orders?

1 button (can't be done!) _____   7 buttons _____

2 buttons _____   8 buttons _____

3 buttons _____   9 buttons _____

4 buttons _____   10 buttons _____

5 buttons _____   11 buttons _____

6 buttons _____   12 buttons _____

Is there more than one way to fill some of these orders?

Button, Button, Where Is The Button?

THIS IS ABOUT

Δ   ordinal numbers

Δ   logic

Δ   language

YOU WILL NEED

Δ   ten small paper cups (small Dixie cups) or large water bottle lids

Δ   one button (needs to fit under lid or cup)

Δ   permanent marking pen or stickers of various kinds

GETTING READY

The idea is to talk about *before* and *after* and to create strategies for making less guesses.

Younger children can do this using only three cups with stickers or shapes on them.

For older children, write the numbers on each cup, and line them up in order. You might want to start with five cups and add more as your child gets comfortable with the activity.

Try lining up the cups in a column instead of a line. Then you can use the terms *above* or *below*.

FAMILY MATH for Young Children

ACTIVITY

1. One of you close your eyes (don't peek!) while the other hides a button under one of the cups.

2. When the button is placed, the other partner's job is to guess under which cup the button is hiding (you can look now).

3. For example: Your partner says : "I think the button is under the third cup." or "I think the button is under cup number three."

   You say, "I put the button under a cup that comes after the third cup."

   Each time talk about which cups are now eliminated. In this case it would be the third cup and all those before it.

   How many guesses did you make before you guessed the correct cup?

4. Play a few rounds taking turns hiding the button.

   The object is to make as few guesses as possible.

   As you repeat the game, you might notice that pretty soon both of you will develop strategies for guessing the correct number with fewer clues.

   What other items can you hide in the cup?

   What other ways can the cups be arranged?

INSIGHT

Some children will identify the positions as next to, over, by, or under. These are excellent and logical answers. As you and your child return to the activity, other words and understanding will evolve.

Measuring Spoons

THIS IS ABOUT

Δ   measuring

Δ   counting

Δ   estimating

YOU WILL NEED

Δ   a set of measuring spoons (use the tablespoon)

Δ   two plastic cups (four to eight ounces)

Δ   some rice or beans

Δ   a die with the numbers from one to three, written twice each (use a die with spots for children who are too young to read numerals), or a spinner like the one in the *Making Spinners* activity

ACTIVITY

1. Give each pair of players one die and one cup.

2. Guess how many tablespoons of rice will fill the cup. You decide if each person can make a guess, or if only one guess is allowed between two players. Write it down.

3. The first person rolls the die and puts that number of tablespoons of rice into the cup.

4. The second person rolls the die and does the same. Do this until the cup is full. How many tablespoonfuls did it take?

What if you used teaspoons?

Try again with each person filling their own cup.

Use different sized cups.

What would happen if you measured water instead of rice? Don't forget to make a guess first!

INSIGHT

Allow guesses to be "adjusted" as the container fills up. This helps develop accuracy in predicting.

Paper Plate Math

This activity was adapted from one by Carol Smith and Anne Linehan.

THIS IS ABOUT

Δ   proportional reasoning

Δ   logical thinking

YOU WILL NEED

Δ   paper plates of two or three colors (or white plates may be colored with crayons or pens)

Δ   scissors

GETTING READY

Think of things from children's lives that can be compared, such as

Δ   food they like

Δ   physical sizes

Δ   values

Δ   parts of a whole (fractions)

Δ   parts of a group

Δ   distances

Have children ask questions or make suggestions about what to compare.

ACTIVITY

1. Mark the center of two plates. Make a slit on each plate from the edge to the center. (If children are able to handle scissors, they should make the cuts themselves.)

2. Match the slits of both plates, and slide them together.

3. Rotate the two plates in opposite directions. Make the two colors get larger or smaller.

4. What happens to one color if the other gets larger? (Be sure you and the child are both looking at the same side of the plates. From the opposite side, the relative sizes of the two colors will be reversed.)

5. Use the plates to compare things.

    "Think about yellow bananas and red apples. Use your plates to show which you like better. How much better do you like that fruit?"

6. If children are having difficulty, help them by asking more questions:

    "Do you like bananas a whole lot better than apples? Can you make the yellow part a whole lot bigger than the red part of the plates?"

For each question, decide which color represents each idea.

Paper Plate Math (continued)

Two-Color Questions:

Allow time for your child to explain the answers. Do only a few at a time. Let your child ask you questions.

How much of each day are you asleep and how much are you awake?

How much time do you wish you could sleep (be awake)?

How much time do you watch TV and how much time do you play outside?

Show how many red and yellow flowers there are.

Show me how much you like summer and winter.

Show me one o'clock (or another time).

Show me something that's more than 1/2 (or another fraction).

Show me 1/3 and 2/3.

Which would you rather play, checkers or dominoes?

How much bigger is your family than your friend's family?

Tell me a story using your paper plates.

When you have worked with two plates for a while, add another plate and make up new questions.

Three-Color Questions:

Show me how much you like the three colors of your plates.

How much do you enjoy playing ball, reading books, or helping clean up?

Show me how much time you spend at school, sleeping, and at the playground.

Show me which go faster: cars, dogs, or turtles.

Tracing Shapes

THIS IS ABOUT

Δ   shapes

Δ   design

Δ   patterns

YOU WILL NEED

Δ   paper

Δ   various-sized lids, blocks, cookie cutters, medium-size puzzle pieces and other assorted traceable items

Δ   crayons, chalk, pencils, or markers

ACTIVITY

1.   Choose some items to trace on the paper.

2.   Tell each other a story about the shapes you traced.

Which shapes have straight sides?

Which shapes have curved sides?

Which shape was the hardest to trace?

What other things can you trace?

Can you make a pattern with your shapes? Here's a pattern that Leti made for her mom:

INSIGHT:

Tracing helps your child's fine (small) muscle development. Tracing skills develop gradually, so don't be surprised at the detours your child might take. This activity also involves making choices about what to trace, and comparing the various shapes. Four-year olds love to trace their hands (and yours)!

Mixtures — Bean Salads and Fish Bowls

This activity was contributed by Ann Carlyle, based on one by Ernestine Camp. It is appropriate for children seven years and older.

THIS IS ABOUT

Δ   numbers

Δ   pre-algebra

Δ   logic

YOU WILL NEED

Δ   beans or markers of various colors (those mentioned in the bean problems are black beans, red beans, and lima beans, but other kinds may be substituted)

Δ   a "salad bowl" or "fish bowl" or place to put the beans

GETTING READY

Each of the salads or fish bowls is a number problem.

Each has two kinds of beans or fish.

Work together to find the solutions.

If the problems seem too hard, put this activity aside for later. There are samples appropriate for four to six year-olds in Part 3 of this activity.

Somebody says we're supposed to be teaching our kids "algebra" when they are little?!!

You mean like a+b=c? It's just getting some ideas about algebra and numbers. Here's an example:

"The number of black beans is twice the number of red beans, and there are 6 beans in all."

Now ask yourself these questions: Are there more black beans or red beans?

> *black*

If I put 1 red bean in the salad, how many black beans would I put in?

> *2*

Does that add up to 6?

> *no*

If I put in 1 more red bean, how many black beans should I add?

> *2*

Does that add to 6?

> *yes*

Later, when we get ready for algebra, we might say:

> *Let "r" stand for the number of red beans.*
>
> *Then (since there are twice as many black beans) "2r" stands for the number of black beans.*
>
> *And r + 2r = 6 (or 3r = 6)*

ACTIVITY 1: TWO BEAN SALADS

Work together to find out what's in each salad. Each one has two kinds of beans. Some salads may have more than one answer.

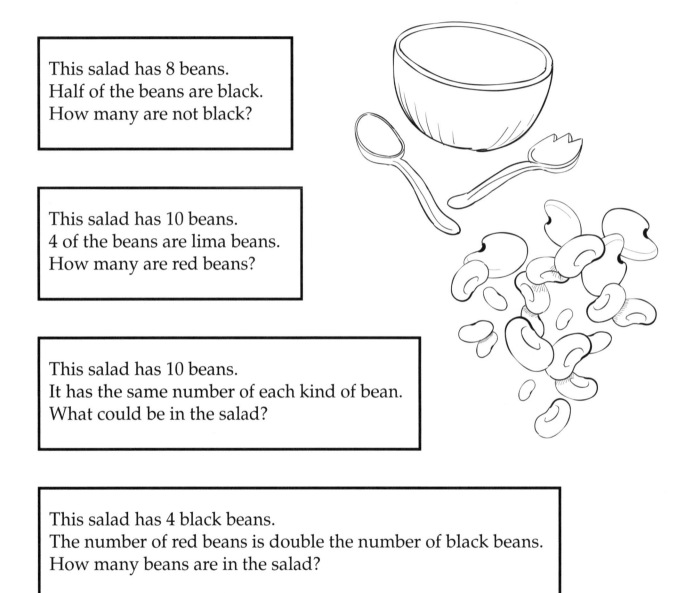

This salad has 8 beans.
Half of the beans are black.
How many are not black?

This salad has 10 beans.
4 of the beans are lima beans.
How many are red beans?

This salad has 10 beans.
It has the same number of each kind of bean.
What could be in the salad?

This salad has 4 black beans.
The number of red beans is double the number of black beans.
How many beans are in the salad?

There are 5 lima beans and 2 more red beans than lima beans.
How many red beans are there?

FAMILY MATH for Young Children

There are 5 beans in all.
There is 1 more lima bean than red beans.
How many of each kind?

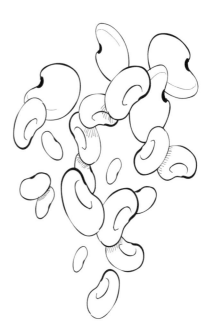

There are 6 lima beans.
There are 3 more red beans than lima beans.
How many beans in the salad?

There are 6 beans in all.
There are half as many lima beans as red beans.
Describe this salad.

There are 4 beans in all.
There are three times as many black beans as red beans.
How many of each color?

There are 5 lima beans and 2 less red beans than lima beans.
How many red beans are there?

ACTIVITY 2: TWO-FISH BOWLS

Each fish bowl has two kinds of fish.

This bowl has 5 fish.
There are 3 goldfish.
How many catfish are there?

This bowl has 5 goldfish.
There is 1 less catfish than goldfish.
How many catfish are there?

This bowl has 4 catfish,
and 1 more goldfish than catfish.
How many fish are there?

This bowl has 4 goldfish,
and an equal number of catfish.
How many fish are there?

Create your own fish bowl combinations.

FAMILY MATH for Young Children

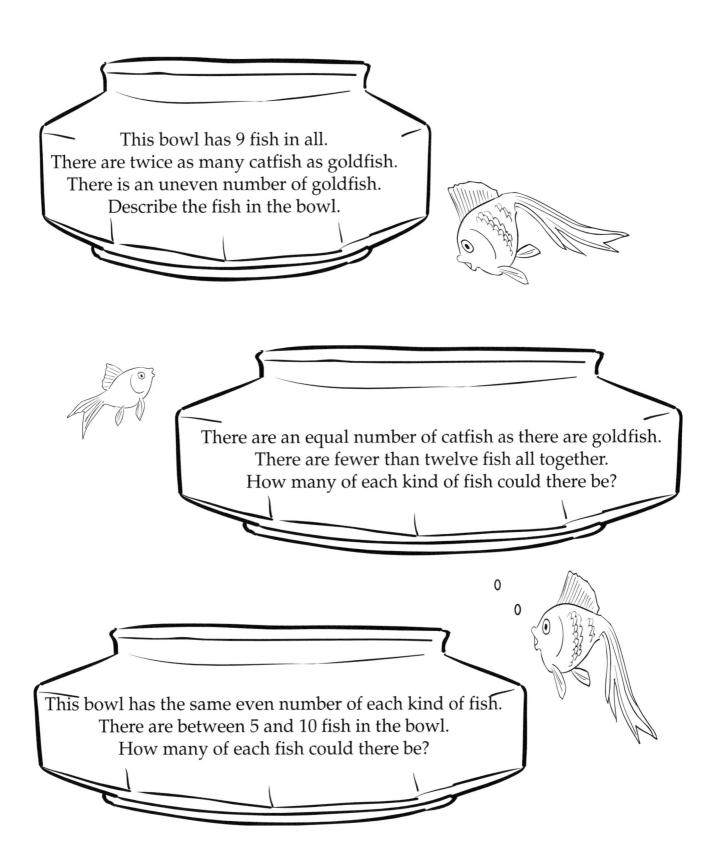

This bowl has 9 fish in all.
There are twice as many catfish as goldfish.
There is an uneven number of goldfish.
Describe the fish in the bowl.

There are an equal number of catfish as there are goldfish.
There are fewer than twelve fish all together.
How many of each kind of fish could there be?

This bowl has the same even number of each kind of fish.
There are between 5 and 10 fish in the bowl.
How many of each fish could there be?

ACTIVITY 3: MAKING SALADS

1. Work together to make up bean salads.

2. Start out with just two kinds of beans or markers, and two cups. Add more beans and more cups as you wish.

3. Into each cup, put a few of one or two kinds of beans. (Be sure to start with small numbers.)

4. Write down some facts or clues about the beans.

For ages four to six: Start with these. Arrange the beans as you tell the story.

I have 2 black beans. (Put two beans on the table.)
Each black bean has two lima beans next to it. (Let your child place two lima beans next to each black bean.)
How many lima beans are there? (Count them using a puppet or doll, ask your child if the puppet counted correctly.)

There are 3 lima beans in my soup. (Place three lima beans on a plate.)
There is 1 red bean for each lima bean. (Place a red bean next to each lima bean.)
How many beans are there? (You count them aloud and ask your child if you counted them correctly.)

Every time I put a red bean in the pot, (Place one red bean "in the pot".)
2 black beans have to be added. (Have your child add two beans each time.)
I have 4 red beans.
How many black beans are there?

Have your child make up a mixture for you to solve. Children enjoy being the teacher.

Here are some examples of the kinds of things you could say. These sentences don't add up to a problem that you can solve. They are just ideas.

Use other words, too. Make the descriptions so that you and your family can understand them.

◊   There are two red beans.

◊   There are three red beans and one black bean.

◊   There are an equal number of red beans and black beans.

◊   There are four more black beans than red beans.

◊   There are two less (or fewer) lima beans than red beans.

◊   There are 10 beans in all.

◊   There is a total of 6 beans.

◊   This salad has 12 beans.

◊   Half (or 1/3 or 1/4) of the beans are lima beans.

◊   Five beans make up half of the salad.

◊   There are 3 times as many pinto beans as white beans.

◊   The number of red beans is double that of white beans.

◊   There is the same number (or an equal number) of lima beans and red beans.

When you have a description that makes a good problem, take your beans away and let someone else solve the problem.

BEAN SOUP FOR SHANELLE: KINDERGARTEN ALGEBRA

Shanelle is six years old. This conversation took place the first time she tried making bean salads with her Grandma.

Grandma: We are going to make some bean salads. Each salad has to have two kinds of beans. We have pinto beans and black beans.

Shanelle: Can we make bean soup instead?

Grandma: Sure we can. This soup has four pinto beans. For every pinto bean there are two black beans.

Shanelle: You mean each pinto bean needs two black beans?

Grandma: Yes, that is another way to say it. (Shanelle lines up four pinto beans and places two black beans next to each one.)

Grandma: Now, here is my question. How many black beans are there in this soup?

Shanelle: Let me count them. (She counts.) There are eight black beans. Can we do another one?

Grandma: Of course. Shall I make a recipe, or do you want to?

Shanelle: You make it.

Grandma: OK, there are ten beans altogether. There are the same number of pinto beans as there are black beans.

Shanelle: That's easy! (She lines up ten pinto beans.) Ten!

Grandma: OK. There are ten pinto beans. Can we add the black beans now?

Shanelle: Oops. I have a way to do this. (She removes five pinto beans and places a black bean between each pinto bean. She counts the beans to make sure there are ten and then pairs them up to make sure there are the same number of beans). There you go, five and five of each.

Grandma: Shanelle, you amaze me!

Shanelle: Can I make a recipe for you now?

Grandma: I'd love it!

Shanelle: There are seven pinto beans. There are five black beans for each pinto bean.

Grandma: (Arranges the beans in seven rows, each beginning with a pinto bean, followed by five black beans.) OK, Here's my bean soup. Is this what you meant?

Shanelle: Let's count them. (She counts each row of black beans.) Yes, but here is my question. How many are there altogether?

Grandma: Let's see that's thirty-five black beans, plus seven pinto beans. That's forty-two altogether.

Shanelle: Very good, grandma! You know how to add big numbers!

Shanelle preferred bean soup to bean salad, so soup it was! Whenever Shanelle goes to her grandma's house, she asks, "Where are the math beans?"

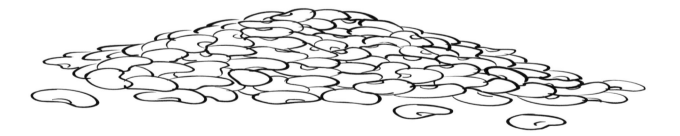

I'm a Shape

THIS IS ABOUT

Δ   making shapes

Δ   using big muscles

Δ   developing a feel for space

YOU WILL NEED

Δ   yourselves

GETTING READY

This is another good activity for taking a break. Make it as active as possible, outdoors if you can.

Moving around helps develop a sense of space. We sometimes like children to sit down and behave and do small muscle activities, such as writing or coloring, but "moving big muscles" seems to have a connection to later learning. It's very important.

Last week Robert's teacher shared a photo of him catching a ball. What does that have to do with learning?

I've heard that the development of children's coordination and using big muscles is an important part of being ready to learn.

Come to think of it, his teacher did say his coordination was improving. I guess all this running, jumping, and galloping about is really important.

ACTIVITY

1. Stand side by side or across from each other.

2. One person makes a shape with her or his arms, such as a circle.

3. The other person makes the same shape.

4. On the next turn, the second person makes a shape, maybe with his or her arms, legs or whole body. Be imaginative!

5. Keep on taking turns, making different shapes, until somebody gets tired or until you are out of time.

6. Try "drawing" the shapes in the air with your elbow, or your nose. Make a pattern of the movements and you've got a dance! For example:

    Make a circle with your shoulder, a triangle with your hand, and two straight lines with your foot. Spin around once, and repeat the pattern three times.

    Try your new dance to some music you enjoy.

    Take turns creating new moves.

Here are some shapes to try:

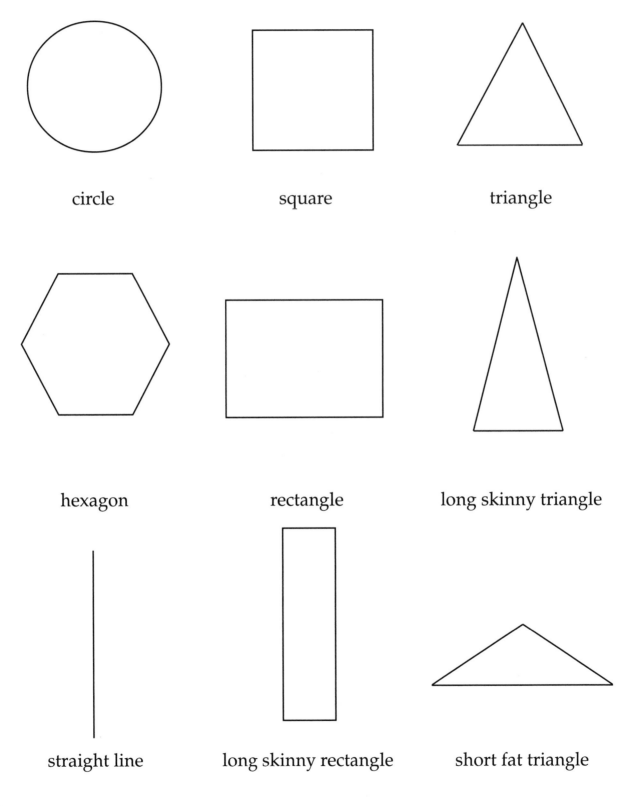

circle   square   triangle

hexagon   rectangle   long skinny triangle

straight line   long skinny rectangle   short fat triangle

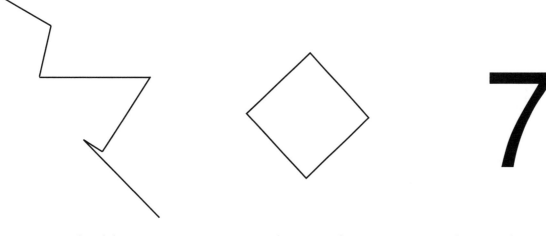

crooked line   diamond   shape of a number

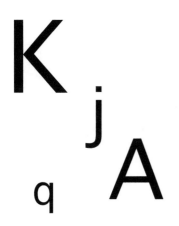

letters of the alphabet   Make up your own

Moon and Stars

THIS IS ABOUT

Δ   patterns

Δ   shapes

Δ   observing change

YOU WILL NEED

Δ   scissors

Δ   string or yarn

Δ   paper in various colors or

Δ   recycled greeting cards or calendars

GETTING READY

Invite your child to look at the moon with you. Keep track of the different phases of the moon. You can do this by looking at it every night and making a simple illustration on your calendar. Some calendars have the moon in all its phases on them.

ACTIVITY

1.   When you have three or four different shapes of the moon, draw them on cardboard or white paper and cut them out.

2.   Cut out some star shapes.

3.   Trace and cut out as many stars and moons as you like and lay them out in a pattern.

FAMILY MATH for Young Children

4. When your child has created a pattern, string the moon and star shapes together. Let your child pick a special place to hang them.

Investigating Patterns:

☆ If you have three moons and six stars, what kinds of patterns could you create? What if you doubled that amount?

☆ What other patterns can you create?

☆ Does the moon really change its shape?

☆ Design some suns and add them to your patterns.

More Fun

Write the names of each member of your family on a star or a moon. Arrange them in a pattern. For instance, you could line them up from oldest to youngest.

INSIGHT

Children create simple patterns at first (A, B, A, B) and move onto more complex patterns as they mature and gain experience. There are patterns everywhere in mathematics and science. Learning to see them and to create them will help your child be a successful probelm solver.

Same Yet Different

THIS IS ABOUT

Δ   sorting

Δ   sets (groups)

YOU WILL NEED

Δ   a collection of like items: such as 10 toys, 5 books, 8 rocks, or 9 shells

ACTIVITY

1. Place the toys in a row and decide silently which toys to separate based on common characteristics. For example: There are eight toys and three are cars with wheels. Separate the cars from the rest (just move them forward) of the toys and ask your child to guess your rule.

2. The second person tries to guess what the characteristics are. In this case there are eight toys and three of them have wheels.

3. The second person creates a set and the first person tries to guess the common elements.

ACTIVITY

If the child finds a common characteristic is different than the one you have in mind, accept and add, "Yes, that works."

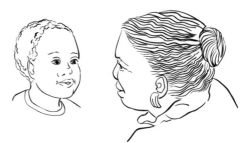

If your child has trouble guessing your "rule", do not say that it is wrong, simply ask another question. "Hm-mmm, I did not see that. What else do you notice?"

INSIGHT

Children learn to ask questions and stay open to learning when they are encouraged and motivated.

Many Shapes

THIS IS ABOUT

Δ   making shapes

Δ   comparing sizes and shapes

YOU WILL NEED

Δ   cardboard or heavy colored paper

Δ   scissors

Δ   pen or pencil

Δ   straightedge or ruler

Δ   jar lids or other circular objects

GETTING READY

Work together with children to draw paper shapes and cut them out. The shapes don't have to be perfect. A lopsided square is OK. A circle that's not quite round is OK too. Use jar lids to help with the circles.

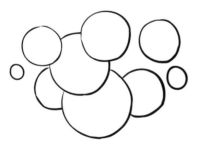

You'll be asked to compare some of your shapes. If you can't tell which shape is bigger, just guess, but talk about what makes you think one is bigger than another.

What does "bigger" mean? Does it mean longer, or wider, or farther around the edges? All of these might be right sometimes.

We made these shapes and now we need to decide which is bigger. We couldn't be sure, but we think this one is bigger.

It looks that way when we put one on top of the other, but let's see if we can figure out another way to compare. What if we covered each one with beans?

ACTIVITY

1. Draw or trace a bunch of shapes on cardboard or paper and cut them out. Use squares, rectangles, triangles, circles, and any other shapes you like. Make sure that there are some that are larger and some that are smaller.

2. Ask each other questions and explain your answers. For example:

    Which are most alike? In what way?

    How are these two alike or different?

    Which shapes are most different? Why does it seem that way?

    Which is the biggest? smallest?

3. Sort the shapes by the number of corners they have, or put them in a row so that the one with the most corners is at one end and the one with no corners at all is at the other end.

4. Put them in a stack so that the largest is on the bottom, the next largest is next to the bottom, and so on until the smallest is on the top.

    How can you decide which is bigger?

    Make up other challenges for yourself.

INSIGHT

There are many ways to be "correct." Be sure to allow for unusual answers. Encouraging your child to be a creative thinker will develop problem-solving skills.

Love Notes Quilt Patch

THIS IS ABOUT

Δ   patterns

Δ   shapes

Δ   spatial reasoning

YOU WILL NEED

Δ   some crayons, pencils

Δ   glue stick or paste

Δ   scissors

Δ   paper, 8-inch squares (to make designs on) or recycled wrapping paper

Δ   cardboard squares

GETTING READY

Are there quilts in your family? In some families quilts are created and passed on from generation to generation. Sometimes quilts are displayed as art, others are carefully preserved in hope chests, and some are used every day. This activity is about creating a quilt patch called Love Notes.

ACTIVITY

Creating a quilt takes planning and visualizing (this means seeing things in your mind and imagining how things might go together).

1.   Create some different designs on three pieces of paper. Try making the designs in three different sizes: One with a large, one with a medium, and one with a small design on it. For example: large flowers, medium flowers, tiny flowers.

2.   Trace and cut some shapes from the paper you designed for your quilt patch. The pattern on the facing page has all the shapes you will need. You might want to make yours bigger or smaller. It's up to you.

3. What other quilt patches can you create using the same pieces? Try making them.

As you make your designs or quilt patch, talk about what might happen to the design if you flipped the triangles on the long sides or the points. What if you slid them along a straight line, point-to-point? Try it.

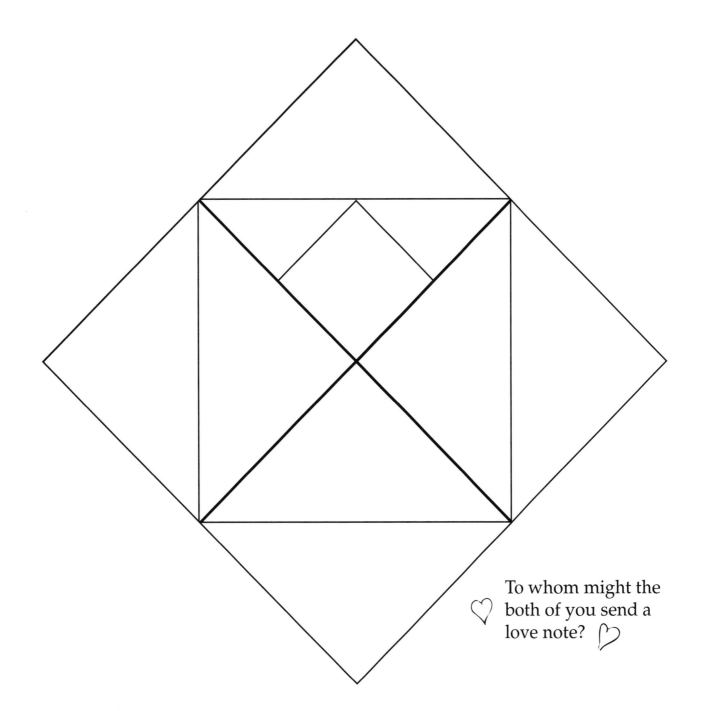

To whom might the both of you send a love note?

Try designing your own family quilt patch.

Think about how many squares, triangles, or other shapes you will need.

OUR FAMILY QUILT PATCH

Name That Shape

THIS IS ABOUT

△ geometry

△ listening

△ describing

YOU WILL NEED

△ shapes: squares, circles, triangles, rectangles, rhomboids

△ a book to serve as a "barrier" to put up so that your partner cannot see what shape you picked

ACTIVITY

1. Look at the shapes together, and talk about what you see.

2. The first person picks a shape and keeps it behind the folder so that the other person cannot see it.

"I am thinking of a shape."
"It has three sides."

"Is it a _____?"

3. The first person then gives clues until the other person guesses correctly.

4. Exchange roles and start over.

INSIGHT

Older children may not need visual clues. Younger children will need to see all the shapes in front of them so that they can compare the verbal clues with the actual shapes.

Patterns All Around

THIS IS ABOUT

Δ   patterns

YOU WILL NEED

Δ   yourselves

ACTIVITY

1. Look around the room and notice the kinds of patterns you see.

    Are there patterns on your clothes?

    Are there wall-paper patterns in the room?

    What patterns do you see on the floor?

    Are there patterns on buildings?

2. Talk about designs you like and create some patterns of your own. Pretend the facing page is your place to design a floor, a piece of fabric, a scarf, a blanket, or anything else that has patterns.

3. Draw a pattern with pictures of things your family likes or enjoys. Show it off, or put it away somewhere special. First, you might want to make a list of things your family likes, or enjoys doing together.

INSIGHT

Color, texture, and pattern are the basic elements for creating textiles. Someone has an idea they want to convey, and creates symbols which are then arranged in patterns.

Our Own Pattern Design

Make-a-Pair

THIS IS ABOUT

Δ   observing

Δ   remembering

Δ   comparing numbers

Δ   adding numbers

YOU WILL NEED

Δ   a set of Make-a-Pair cards (See pages 103-104.)

GETTING READY

Make copies of the Make-a-Pair cards, on a copy machine or by drawing pictures on cardboard squares, and cut them apart.

Mix the cards and put them face down in a rectangular arrangement.

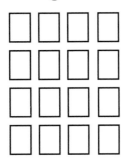

For younger children, start with just six cards (three pairs) in an array.

I always just guess when I play games like Make-a-Pair.

That's okay, it's a start. But let's see if we can practice remembering where the cards are. We don't have to be perfect, you know!

Oh, boy! I remember where that one is! I got one!

ACTIVITIES

Pairs

This is a warm-up game to practice matching. Start with the deck of Make-a-Pair cards, face down.

1. Take turns turning over one card at a time. Leave it face up.

    If the card you turn over matches a card that is already turned over, you get to remove both cards.

2. Continue taking turns until all the cards have been matched.

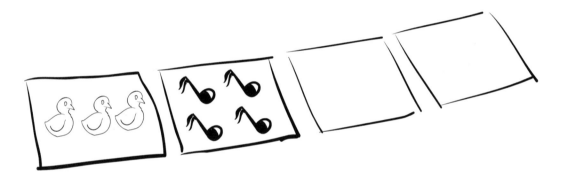

Mini-Pairs

1. Set out six cards in a rectangle, face down. (Be sure there are three matching pairs.)

2. Take turns turning over one card at a time. Leave it face up.

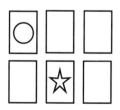

3. If the new card turned over matches one of those already face up, take both cards and put them aside.

    How many turns will it take to match all six cards?

Make-a-Pair (continued)

Hidden Matches

1. Take turns turning over two cards.

2. If your two cards are a match, keep them.

3. If your two cards do not match, look carefully to remember where they are, then turn them face down again, in the same place where they were.

4. On your next turn, try again to find a match. Try to remember the cards that you already know.

5. Continue taking turns until all the cards have been matched.

Match for Five

1. Put all the cards face up, so you can see them.

2. On each turn, pick up two or three cards that add to five.

3. Continue until all of the cards have been matched, or until you can't make five anymore.

FAMILY MATH for Young Children

Make-a-Pair Cards

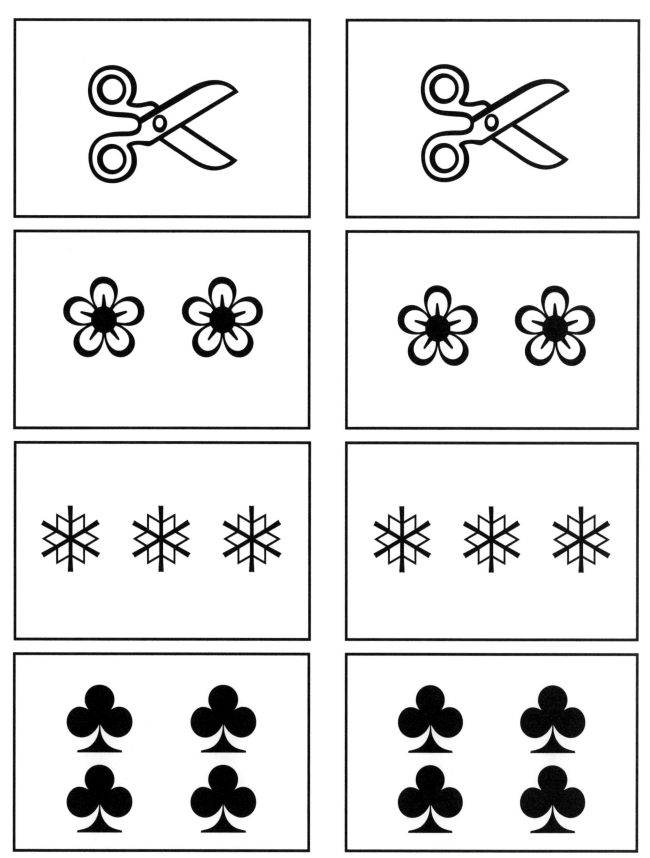

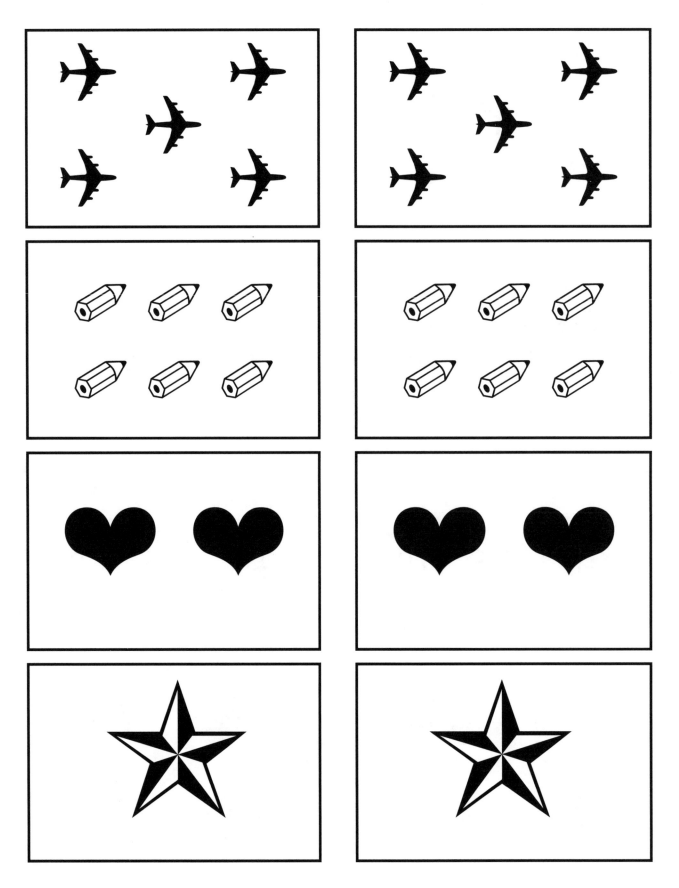

FAMILY MATH for Young Children

Looking at Letters

THIS IS ABOUT

Δ   observing

Δ   learning to recognize letters and numbers

YOU WILL NEED

Δ   scissors

Δ   a blank sheet of paper

Δ   make a copy of the big letters on the following pages

Δ   a blank card (one that you can't see through)

GETTING READY

This activity is better for children who are reading or beginning to read. They need to be able to recognize all the letters when they see the whole figure. For children who cannot identify letters or numbers yet, try using pictures of animals or toys.

Cut apart the letters on the pages you copied, so they are like a deck of cards. Mix them up, and stack them face up. Be sure all the tops point the same way. Put the blank card on top of the stack.

You know, I never really looked at the parts of letters before. How interesting!

Yes, look how many are round on top, and how many are flat!

And which ones just have one line pointing up at the top!

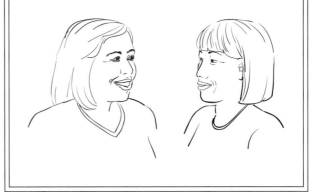

ACTIVITY

Slo-o-o-owly pull the blank card down from the top, so that you can see the tip-top of the letter. Keep pulling the blank card down slowly. Each time you stop, talk about which letters they could be. Continue until you can be sure what letter it is. You may want to keep the book open to the page of letters.

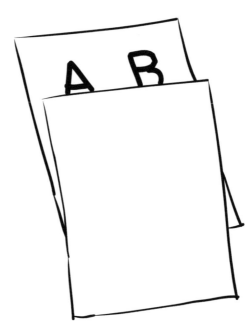

Things To Talk About

Which letters can you guess right away?

Which letters can you not see until you get to the middle?

Which letters can you not guess until you get to the very bottom?

Where were you able to guess for the letter E? Which other letter might it have been before the bottom line?

Try pulling the blank card up from the bottom.

What about if you pulled the blank card from left to right?

Some letters are symmetric, or the same on both sides or on top and bottom. Are symmetric letters easier or harder to guess?

Use these letters and numbers for **Looking at Letters** and other activities.

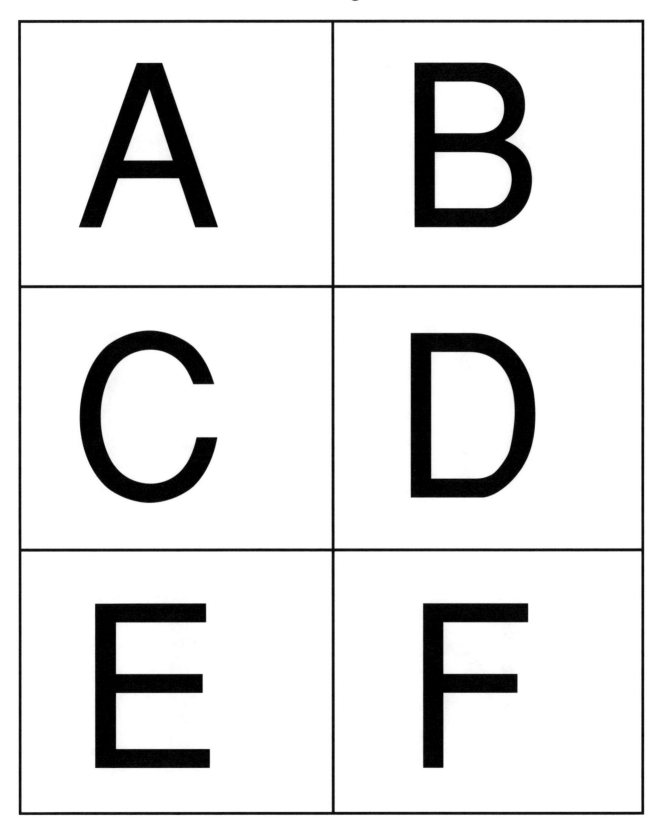

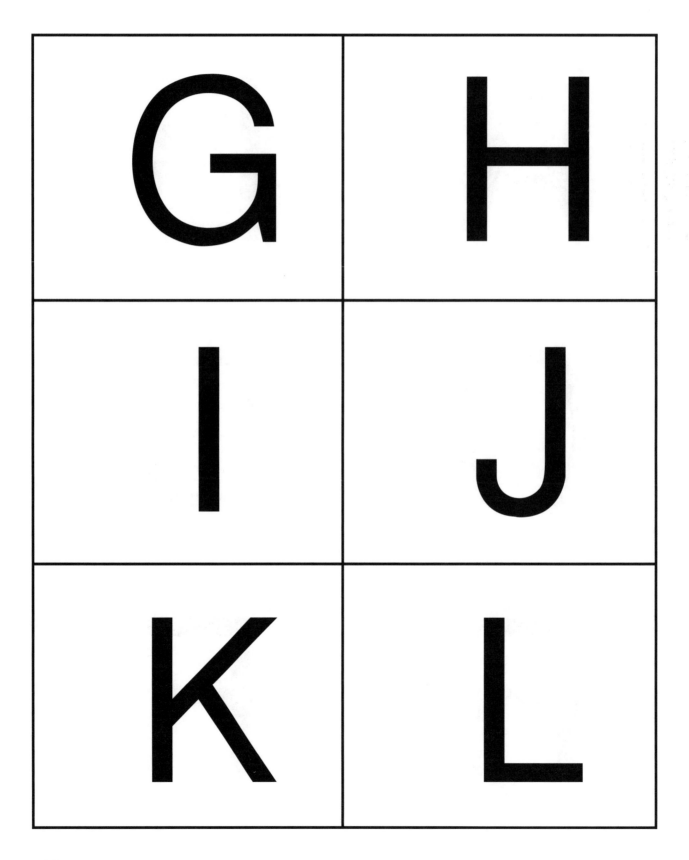

FAMILY MATH for Young Children

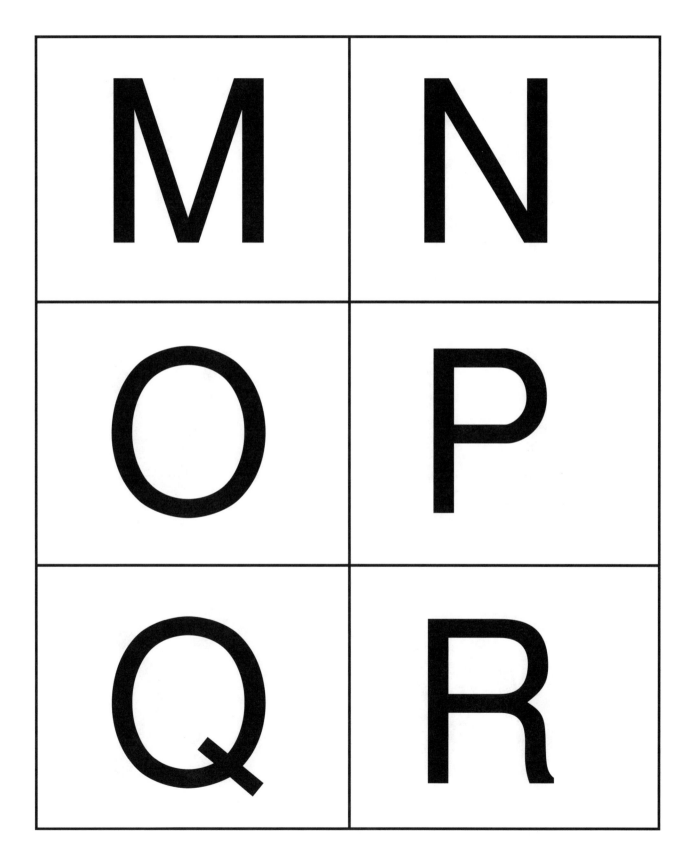

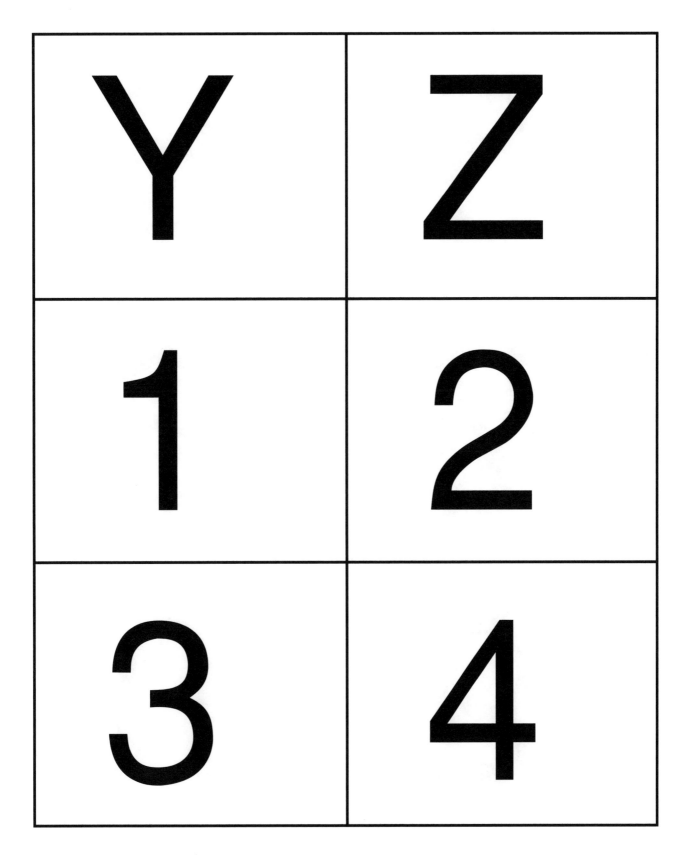

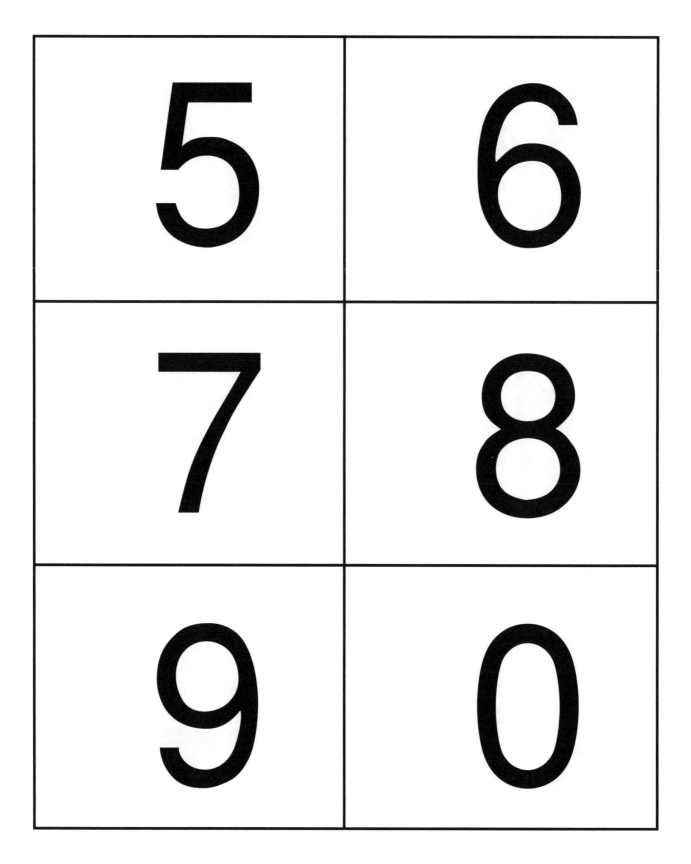

FAMILY MATH for Young Children

Here is a page of mixed letters and numbers to try.

Cover the page, and pull the paper down one row at a time.

Compare what you see of each letter or number.

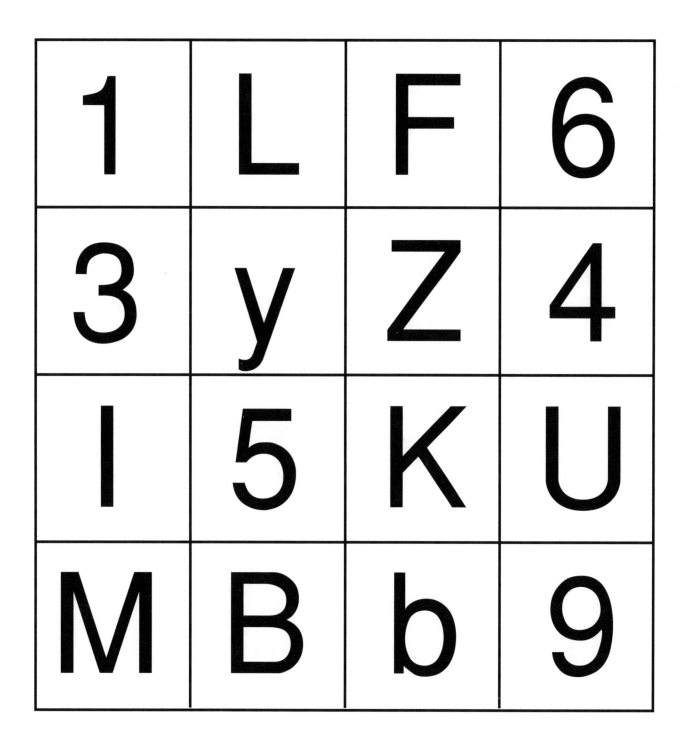

Tell Me What You See

THIS IS ABOUT

Δ   observing

Δ   describing details

YOU WILL NEED

Δ   a variety of materials, such as
    rocks, plants, small toys, kitchen
    utensils, writing tools, pictures
    of various animals and objects

GETTING READY

This is about using words and
communicating. Be sure there is lots
of conversation back and forth.

Try asking questions about the
outdoors, about plants, buildings, or
animals.

*"Tell me what you see in front of us.
How would you describe it?"*

*"It's big, and has green leaves, and
brown on the bottom."*

"What else?"

*"It makes a sound when the wind
blows, and it shades the sunshine,
and it doesn't ever move to a different
place."*

ACTIVITY

1. Choose an object. Put the object, perhaps a pot or pan, on the table for the child to look at.

2. Say, "Tell me everything you can about this. Tell me what you see."

3. The child will probably tell you what the object is used for, and that's fine.

   To help him or her get started on the description, ask some questions, such as:

   "What does this part look like?"

   "Is it shiny or dull?"

   "Is it hard or soft when you touch it?"

   "What shapes do you see?"

   "What colors does it have?"

   "What about this other part? How is it different from this part?"

   "Right now, does it feel hot or cold?"

   "What do you think it is used for?"

   "What else could it be used for?"

   "What else can you tell me about it?"

   "What other thing is like this?"

5. Keep it fun, not work. Don't spend more than five or ten minutes at one time. Introduce another object later. Don't feel you have to ask all of these questions at one sitting.

6. After a while, have the child think of questions to ask you about an object.

INSIGHT

These activities will help children become aware of the characteristics of objects and be able to use words to describe similarities and differences.

What's Alike About You and Me?

THIS IS ABOUT

Δ   observing and comparing

YOU WILL NEED

Δ   paper and pencil

ACTIVITY

1.   Talk together about the ideas of alike and different.

2.   You might want to talk about:

   ☆   sizes

   ☆   things you like to eat

   ☆   different types of hair

   ☆   what you do every day

   ☆   places you have been

   ☆   animals you have seen

   ☆   or anything else.

Hey, Mom, I'm shorter than you, but I know how I can get to be bigger.

How's that?

If I stand on my chair, I'm taller than you! See?!

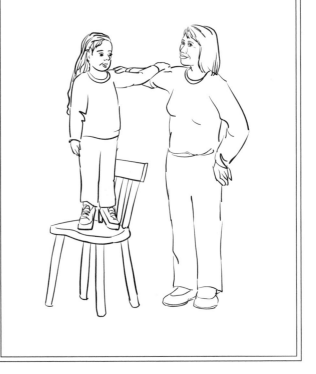

What's alike about you and me? Write or draw a list of as many things as you can think of.	What's different about you and me? Write or draw a list of as many things as you can think of.

What other things did you come up with to compare?

What other ways can you show this information?

Me and My Toys

THIS IS ABOUT

Δ   comparing sizes

Δ   developing understanding of
       length

Δ   getting a feeling for one's own
       space

YOU WILL NEED

Δ   adding machine tape or string

Δ   masking or clear tape

GETTING READY

This activity is fun, and gives
children some experience in
measuring, without having to be too
serious about it.

The figures can be decorated as you
wish. Some people like to add circles
to show their waists or their heads.
Adding feet is fun, too.

*I wish my bear were as big as I am! I
wonder how long his arms would be
then?*

*Well, I like my doll just the size she is.
How would I ever carry around a doll
as big as I am?*

ACTIVITY

1. Use adding machine tape to carefully measure each person's height. Tape the strip to the wall, so that it touches the floor.

2. Check by having the person stand next to his or her strip.

3. Add your arms. To measure armspan, spread out your arms so they go straight across, then measure from fingertips to fingertips.

4. Tape the arms in place across the "height strips."

5. Do the same for teddy bears, dolls, or other toys. Tape their figures next to those of the smallest person, or next to that of the owner of the toy.

How do the large and small figures compare?

Decorate your figures with feet, heads, or fingers.

The figures can be put in a row.

Or, if there is not enough wall space they can be put in "single file."

How would you measure a truck?

This is In and This is Not

THIS IS ABOUT

△   observing

△   describing

△   sorting into categories

YOU WILL NEED

Almost anything will do for this activity, such as:

△   kitchen utensils

△   cans of food

△   empty cans

△   handkerchiefs

△   toys

△   tools

△   beans, blocks, bottlecaps, and so on...

△   string or paper to make the "IN" space.

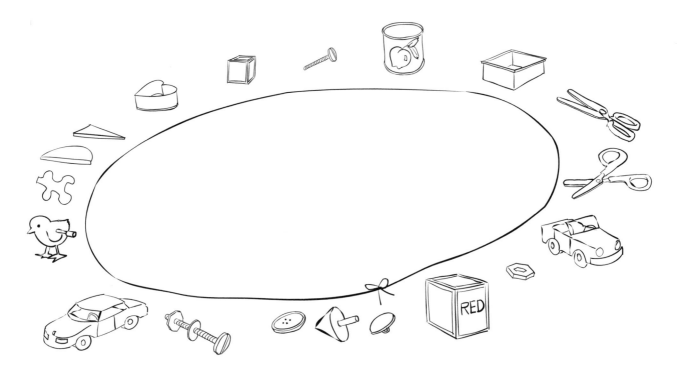

FAMILY MATH for Young Children

GETTING READY

Sorting is usually considered a very important activity for young children. It gives an opportunity to practice observing, describing, and making distinctions between different characteristics.

For older or more experienced children, try using two characteristics, such as "round and hard."

If I sort my cars, I can arrange them in all their different sizes, like this.

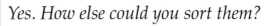

Yes. How else could you sort them?

ACTIVITY

1. Make an "IN" space with a piece of paper or with a string circle. The size will depend on the objects you are using.

2. Have about half a dozen objects for the first game. You might want to start with some small toys.

3. Take turns. For the first game, a grown-up should begin. After that, children may want to start.

4. Think about the items you have, and decide what characteristic you want to use. Choose something that some of the objects have, but others would not. For example, say you had a doll, a teddy bear, a toy truck, a jack-in-the-box, a stuffed giraffe, and a doll-house chair. You could start by picking up the bear and putting it into the IN space, saying, "This is IN because it has hair or fur."

5. Then ask a child to take a turn choosing a toy. Ask if it has hair or fur. If it does, then it goes IN. If it doesn't, then it is NOT IN. Repeat the phrase, "This is IN (or NOT IN) because…"

Continue until all the objects have been sorted.

Use comparisons such as:

Big or not big	Hard or not hard
Fuzz or no fuzz	New or not new
Mine or not mine	To eat or not to eat
Sticky or not sticky	A toy or not a toy
Light-colored or not	Heavy or not heavy
Long or not long	Rolls or won't roll
Noisy or not noisy	A tool or not a tool
Red or not red	

And use your imagination for many more IN things!!

What Is Missing?

THIS IS ABOUT

Δ   counting

Δ   remembering

YOU WILL NEED

Δ   a partner, although you can do this with several people

Δ   about five to ten small items or toys

ACTIVITY

This is a kid version of a popular baby shower game.

1.   Sit on the floor with toes touching so that your legs create a border around a space where you will place three or four toys…

… or make space on the table and create an enclosed or bordered area — you can use yarn, string, or a tray.

Let's see if you can tell which one I took away. Close your eyes. No peeking!

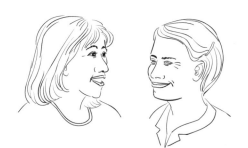

O.K., you can look now. Can you tell which thing is missing?

Is it the car?

Yes it is! Now you take one and I will guess.

Hmm… let's see — I think I remember a comb. No, there's the comb. Could it be the shell?

2.   Place three or four items in the enclosed space. You can use a few more with older children. Say the name of each item as you place it.

3.   Ask your child to tell you what each item is.

4.   Have your child close his eyes. No peeking!

5.   Take one item and hide it behind you, or put it in a bag.

6.   Now let your child see what is left and guess what is missing. After a couple of guesses, give hints like: "It has four legs." or "It is red."

7.   Close your eyes and have your child remove one toy and hide it. As you look to see what is missing, you might think aloud. "Let's see, I remember there was something with wheels."

For Fun

You can increase the game's difficulty for older children by increasing the number of objects or decreasing the differences between the objects. For example, you can use only matchbox cars or only pencils.

Children love this game. They will enjoy playing it over and over. Also, they prefer the version where their toes are touching your toes.

My Rule, Your Rule

THIS IS ABOUT

Δ   sorting

Δ   likeness and difference

Δ   counting

YOU WILL NEED

Δ   small objects for sorting:

        buttons   keys
        small toys   bottle caps
        picture cards seashells
        play money   etc.

Δ   sorting spaces:

        paper plates
        sheets of paper
        small boxes

GETTING READY

This is an extension of the idea in *This is In and This is Not* with the addition of slightly more formal rules.

The example, with buttons, uses two characteristics — buttons and four holes. With younger children you might want to have only one characteristic.

Use your creativity to think up new and different sorting activities, with things you have available. It can be sorting different kinds of rocks, or foods, or toys, or — well, you think of other things.

ACTIVITY

In this example, we're using buttons. You may use almost any other materials small enough to be handled.

1. Take a handful of buttons. Think of a rule, such as buttons with four holes. Say, "I'm thinking of a rule. Imagine you can read my mind to guess the rule. I'll put something into the sorting space that fits my rule (put a four-holed button into the sorting space). What do you think my rule is?"

2. If the response is "button," say "That's part of the rule. What else could it be?" and put another four-holed button in the space. Continue until you are satisfied that the idea has been understood, but if it becomes frustrating, leave it for another day.

3. For the next turn, let the child think of a rule and put an object into the sorting space, while you guess the rule or rules.

For some turns, instead of saying what you think the rule is, simply put down another item, and ask "Does this fit the rule?" This helps with getting information and making guesses without "blurting out" the answer. Encourage children to try this method of presenting their guesses.

Return to this activity many times, using different materials.

Make a Game

THIS IS ABOUT

Δ   planning

Δ   numbers

Δ   probability

Δ   following paths

YOU WILL NEED

Δ   dice with the numbers 1, 2 and 3. Each number should appear twice on a die. Or, you can make a spinner like the one in the *Making Spinners* activity.

Δ   strips of paper (one inch by six inches or two inches by ten inches)

Δ   bottle caps, buttons, or other small items to use as markers

Δ   scissors

Δ   other large pieces of cardboard or paper

ACTIVITY

1.   Cut strips of paper two inches wide and ten inches long (this can vary depending on the size of the game board).

2.   Make lines every two inches and write the numbers 1, 2, 3, 4, 5, so you have strips that look like this:

1	2	3	4	5

3. Now make another strip with the numbers 6, 7, 8, 9, 10 written in the squares.

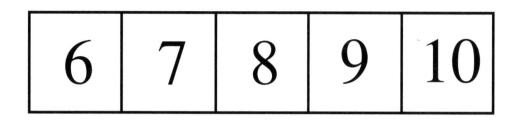

4. Cut out two or three squares that are about the same size as the squares with numbers on them. On these squares you can write stuff like:

5. Use these squares to cover any numbers you choose. Arrange the strips and squares to make a path on the gameboard any way you like. The following page has a sample game.

6. Play a game!

What kind of rules do you want? Keep it simple at first.

Must you roll the exact number to exit the game?

Can you change the rules during the game?

Decide who goes first.

In some games this is decided by rolling the dice and the person with the highest number goes first.

Roll the dice and follow the path. At first you might want to be the first one to get to the end of the path.

Decorate the board — draw or color whatever you want.

Try this sample game if you want to practice first. You can roll dice or make a spinner with numbers from one to three. Decide what markers you will use for playing pieces.

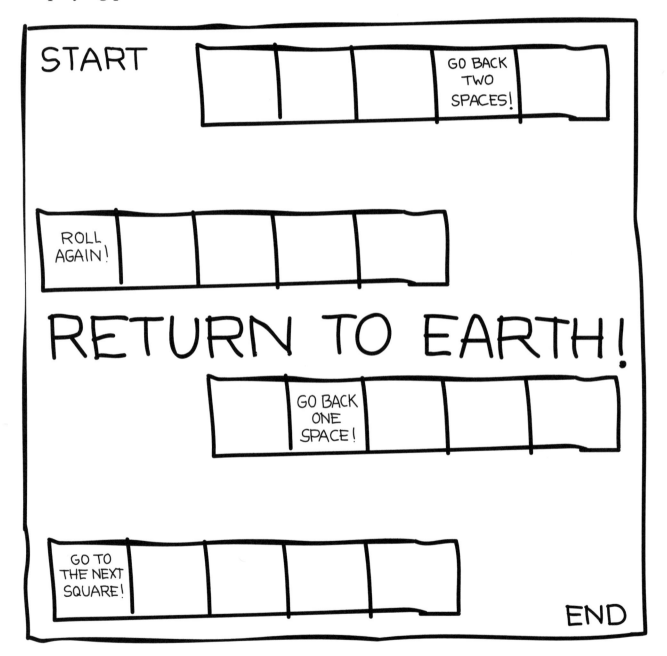

You can try making up other games. Invite your friends and relatives to play with you. Include them in the game!

Make-a-Game Sample

Copy and cut apart

1	2	3	4	5
6	7	8	9	10
11	12	13	14	15
16	17	18	19	20
Move ahead 2 spaces	Lose a turn	Go again	Move back 2 spaces	Move forward 1 space

Making Spinners

YOU WILL NEED

Δ   cardboard

Δ   scissors

Δ   ruler

Δ   pencil

Δ   paper clip

Δ   tape

Δ   hole punch

ACTIVITY

1.   Cut out a cardboard arrow shaped like this:

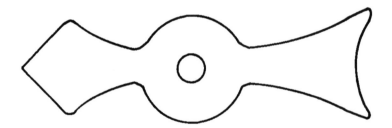

2.   Make a hole in the center, using the hole punch.

3.   Cut a scrap into a small square for a paper washer and use the hole punch to make a hole in the center.

FAMILY MATH for Young Children

4. Cut out a four-inch square of cardboard.

5. On the four-inch card, measure two inches along on all sides and mark lightly.

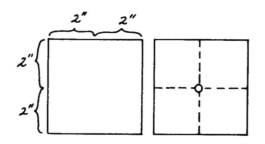

6. Connect these marks with faint pencil lines.

7. Mark the center with a dot.

8. Make a hole in the center of the spinner card with a thumbtack, the pencil point, or the end of the paper clip.

9. Draw a design for the activity you want to do.

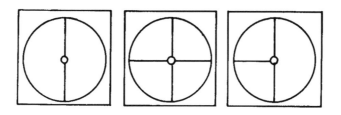

10. Put the bent paper clip through the center hole.

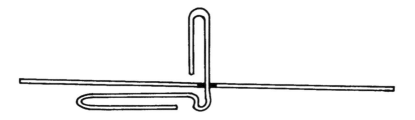

11. First place your washer and then your spinner onto the spinner card and then clip them down.

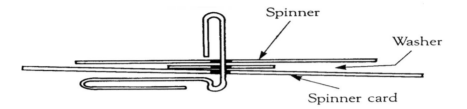

12. Put masking tape on the bottom to hold the paper clip.

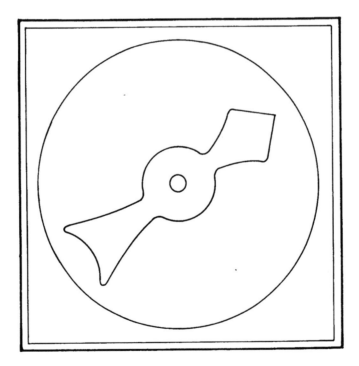

Shadows

THIS IS ABOUT

Δ   looking at shadows to understand space, measurement, and time

YOU WILL NEED

Δ   chalk

Δ   sunshine

Δ   sidewalk or playground

GETTING READY

Think and talk about the kinds of shadows you have seen.

Before you make each shadow, guess how you think it will look.

Think about all the ways you can make changes in the shadows.

You can turn objects in different directions.

With paper, you can twist or fold it.

You can move things closer or farther away from the ground.

Look how tall I am in my shadow! I was short at lunch time. How come?

Interesting — let's keep track of when our shadows are tall and when they are short. Which direction does your shadow go?

It goes that way, and SO DOES YOURS!! Our shadows must like each other.

ACTIVITY

Shadow Fun

On a sunny day, with chalk, work together to make shadow pictures of:

- **Yourselves,** facing away from the sun, facing sideways, dancing, or jumping

  Your hands or your feet

  Your profiles, or your faces from the side

- **A block**
  Move the block in different ways, to look at its different shadows. Can you make it look flat?

- **A hula hoop**
  Turn the hula hoop. Can you make it look flat? oval or round? square?

- **A circle of cardboard**
  Turn it and make different shapes.

- **A triangle of cardboard**
  Is there any way you can make it look round?

- **A pencil**
  How small can you make a pencil look? What happens when you hold it closer or farther from the ground?

- **Use two objects,** and make the shadow of one cover the shadow of the other.

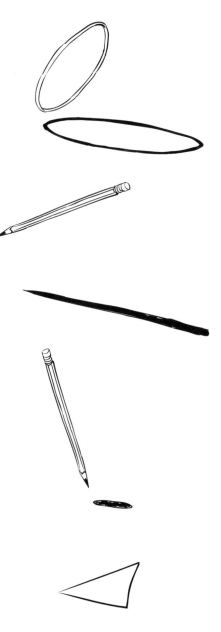

Shadows in Time

Work with a partner.

1. Find a place outside on the playground or sidewalk, where the sun will shine all day — if it's a sunny day, of course!

2. Mark a spot on the ground.

3. About every hour, go stand on that spot and draw an outline of your shadow. What do you see?

Other Things to Try, More Questions to Ask:

Do taller or shorter people make different shadows?

Try it in March and June (or at other times).

Is there a difference at different times of the year?

Try the same with a post or stick stuck in the ground.

Find a sundial to look at. Check it at different times of day. Read about sundials at the library.

In a Secret Treasure Box

In a secret treasure box underneath my bed,
you'll find one thing that is blue
and two that are red.

In a secret treasure box underneath my bed,
there are three things for my fingers
and four for my head.

In a secret treasure box underneath my bed,
I'm saving five things from the ocean
and six that are named Ted.

In a secret treasure box underneath my bed,
there are seven plastic insects
and eight that are quite dead.

In a secret treasure box underneath my bed,
there are nine things from around the world
and ten from my friend Fred.

One treasure is blue,
two are red,
three for my fingers,
four for my head,
five from the ocean,
six named Ted,
seven plastic insects,
eight that are dead,
nine from around the world,
and ten from my friend Fred.

What are those secret treasures?
You might be asking me.
Collect your own and count 'em
and see what yours might be.

Grace Dávila Coates

Collections and Treasures

Collections

Children (and many adults) love to have collections. Sometimes collections begin with a leafy treasure picked up on an afternoon walk or with a gift such as a polished stone. Other collections begin with one special thing brought back from a family weekend or day trip to a park, the beach, or the city. This section is about ordinary things that you and your child may collect just because they interest you or because they remind you of a special moment together.

A collection might include buttons, shells, thread spools, stamps, feathers, pieces from games that are no longer complete, leaves, and piñata or Crackerjack prizes. One child who brought his collection to share had keys from his grandmother's and grandfather's old trunks, houses, and cars. They had collected them over the years, and he knew a story about most of them!

Treasure boxes can be made from shoe boxes, oatmeal boxes, hat boxes, and other "discardables". Tiny treasures can be stored in salt boxes, match boxes, old jewelry boxes, or tea boxes. The main idea is not to spend a lot of money on a box.

Your child can cover the box with recycled wrapping paper, the comics section of a newspaper, or fabric. Japanese and Chinese newspapers make beautiful wrapping. Decorate the box with pieces of twigs, feathers, buttons, art, or ribbon from a long-forgotten craft box.

Collections mean something to the person who owns them. Respect your child's reasons for choosing some things that you may not think are important or special. Listen and look closely. Your child may help you see with "new eyes" as you explore the treasures.

It is important to create a special place for your child's things to keep them safe from intrusion or destruction by other siblings or pets. This helps your child develop a sense of responsibility and accountability.

You might designate a drawer, a shelf, a desk, a bag, or any place that is consistently accessible, and for your child only.

Collections are the perfect beginning for sorting, classifying, counting, tracing, and measurement. The following pages include similar activities using various objects.

Although graphing and sorting mats are included for creating groups or graphing sets, you can also use other materials such as string or yarn to create circles for sorting, old pie tins, fast food boxes, or you can draw your own graphs on pieces of cardboard. Children enjoy creating their own devices for making sense of information.

The following suggestions for exploring mathematics through collections are just the tip of the iceberg. One child created a Treasure Map game by making a grid with letters and numbers on it, just like a map. She remembered a game called Hurkle from a FAMILY MATH class and adapted it. Creating new things from other models is an important skill to develop and nurture.

Let your children create the ideas, games, and conclusions. Ask questions, listen carefully, take your child's ideas seriously, then ask more questions. Above all, have fun!

Stamps Galore!

THIS IS ABOUT

Δ   sorting

Δ   observing

Δ   adding

YOU WILL NEED

Δ   cancelled stamps

Δ   cancelled envelopes

Δ   blank sheet of paper

Δ   magnifying glass (optional)

GETTING READY

Begin a stamp collection. This can be done by recycling the stamps in your daily mail. Have your child collect them with you. You only need about ten or twelve stamps to begin.

If you don't receive much mail, ask friends and family to save their stamps for you.

One person asked her co-workers to save stamps for her — she received hundreds!

ACTIVITY

1. Invite your child to investigate stamps with you.

2. Talk about sending and receiving mail as you look at the various stamps you have collected. Where do you send mail? To whom?

3. You might compare which types of stamps you have the most of, or the least.

4. Have your child chose some stamps to put on an envelope.

5. Talk about why or how the stamps go together. Maybe they were all the same, or they all came from different countries. Maybe they all have flags on them. You decide.

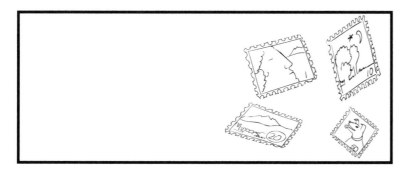

With older children, you might ask them to add the postage on the stamps.

What other ways can you organize the stamps?

Design your own FAMILY STAMP. Who is in it?

Leaf Treasures

THIS IS ABOUT

Δ   estimating

Δ   observing

Δ   language

YOU WILL NEED

Δ   various leaves

Δ   paper

Δ   graph paper (for older children)

Δ   pencils, markers, or crayons

Δ   a paper bag or small box to store leaves

GETTING READY

Go on a leaf-collecting walk. Collect leaves from flowers, trees, or plants.

ACTIVITY

1.   Select a space for spreading out the leaves.

2.   Close your eyes and pick a leaf. Have your child do the same.

3.   Now open your eyes and compare the leaves you have chosen.

     Are your leaves the same color?

     Do they have a different number of points?

     How are they the same?

     How are they different?

     Are there any leaves that are bigger than your hand?

     Are there some types of leaves you have more of than others?

FAMILY MATH for Young Children

What other ways can you sort the leaves into different groups?

Try describing a leaf in every little detail to each other.

For Older Children:

Place your leaf on the graph paper. How many squares do you think your leaf will cover? Trace it and count the actual number of squares it covers completely.

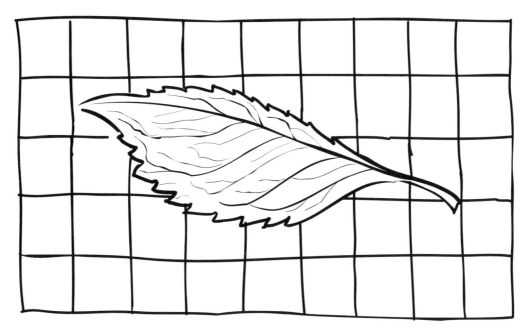

Make A Leaf Book

Research the names of the leaves with your child.

Preserve your leaves so they don't fall apart. Place them between wax paper, or between two cut-out squares of cardboard. Place a heavy book on top to flatten them.

INSIGHT

Collecting and observing things in nature are important science skills. Collecting information and making predictions or estimating are important math skills. Encourage your to child to collect natural objects.

Seashells

THIS IS ABOUT

Δ   creating sets

Δ   number

Δ   quantity

YOU WILL NEED

Δ   some shells

Δ   crayons, pencils, chalk

Δ   paper

GETTING READY

Let your child help you make a roomy space on a counter or table top, so the shells can be observed and sorted.

ACTIVITY

1.   Ask your child to put together some shells that might "go together."

2.   Talk about the different ways sets might be created (color, shape, texture).

Here are some more questions for investigating shells:

What can you tell me about the groups you created?

Can you tell me why you did that?

Are there other possible ways to group them together?

Do we have more of one type of shell than another?

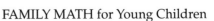

Accept all the answers your child gives. Encourage your child to ask you questions.

Try illustrating some shells; tell something about them that is interesting to you.

Mindy's Shells

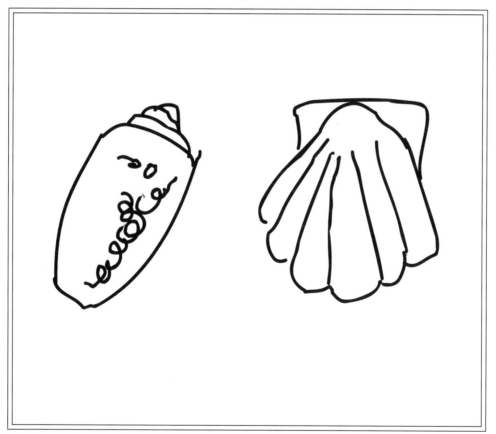

INSIGHT

Observing, comparing, and sorting are important math and science skills. They help us make sense of the world around us. They can be used both for finding patterns in the natural world and for organizing one's work.

Rocks

THIS IS ABOUT

Δ creating sets

Δ number

Δ quantity

YOU WILL NEED

Δ some pebbles, rocks, or stones

Δ crayons

Δ paper

GETTING READY

Collect about twenty rocks or stones. Get some from different places. Rocks near a stream are different from those found by railroad tracks.

If there is a rockery in your area, they might give you samples of the different kinds of rocks they sell.

ACTIVITY 1

1. Spread some rocks out on a tray or flat area and talk about their characteristics.

    Are they cold, warm, smooth, rough?

    What other words describe rocks?

2. Have your child pick one rock to start the set.

3. Now you add a rock to the set and tell why you chose that one. For example: if your child picked a rounded rock, you can add another one that is similar and say, "This belongs because it is round."

4. Next, let your child pick another rock and tell you why it belongs in the set. Remember, they do not all have to be round. Your child may find an interesting connection that you overlooked.

ACTIVITY 2

1. Line up five rocks, choose two that are similar and move them away from the group and say, "There are five rocks and two are smooth."

2. Encourage your child to make a set and make a statement about it.

3. Take turns using different rocks from the bigger set (the twenty rocks you collected).

After you've practiced this for a while, try making up the sets and guess your partner's rules.

How's My Child Doing?

How's My Child Doing?

You know, it's really true that they all develop at different rates, and in different ways!

Mm-hm – mine all took piano lessons, but one was totally serious, the next just played, and the third worked and worked! They all learned to play, too.

Is there anywhere that I can get a checklist that tells how my Joe stacks up, compared to others?

Probably, but that won't help him learn faster or better. How about just watching to see what he does?

I've heard that little kids, up to age eight or nine, need a lot of freedom to explore and play. They say play is children's work!

I agree about the freedom. I think we try too hard to "teach" them things they already know or they're not ready to learn. Besides, have you tried sitting in one place for five hours every day?!!

Aisha says she's keeping a "portfolio" of her work at school. What's that? Should we keep a portfolio at home?

Good idea! It's a folder or box where you put things to save. Maybe her favorites, or your favorites, or something that you can compare with her later work.

Maybe I'll put in some notes of my own, too, about what she's doing. It's easy to forget what they do and how fast they grow.

That's a great idea too! And that way, if you have any worries about her, you can tell the teacher, or a nurse, or her doctor exactly what you see.

What kinds of things should I be looking for?

On the next couple of pages are some ideas. Just remember that it's different for every child and they are always learning, even when they seem to be just playing.

Here are a few activities to try with a child. Try other similar questions, too. Watch closely and you may be surprised. Most of the skills depend on the child's development; over and over it has been proven that they absolutely cannot be rushed.

What you CAN do is give lots of opportunity to play with all kinds of things and to move big muscles, to use their arms and legs and themselves. Avoid too much time sitting, watching, coloring, or doing things just with the hands.

A Question	Something to Try	Things to Look For
Can the child see the difference between two objects?	Hold up a teaspoon and a tablespoon, and ask which is bigger (or smaller).	This understanding will probably develop between ages two and four. Be sure that two objects can be distinguished before you have the child try to put several objects in order.
Can the child match one group of things to another, one-to-one?	Get out four red blocks and four blue blocks. Put the red blocks in a row, with each block separate. Ask the child to match one blue block with each of the red blocks.	This is likely to be difficult for children under age five. Even though they may be able to count by rote, they have trouble seeing the connection between individual blocks and numbers.

154

A Question	Something to Try	Things to Look For
Can the child "conserve" number, or see that they are the same number when the blocks are spread out?	Put four blocks in a row, slightly separated. Have the child count the blocks with you. Separate the blocks so that they make a longer row. Ask whether there are more or fewer blocks now.	Until age five, or even later, most children will not be able to recognize that there are just as many blocks when they are shoved together as there are when they are spread out. This is hard to believe until you see it. It can convince us that children think differently. Don't try to tell or teach a child that the numbers are the same. Give lots of experience with objects, and they will get the idea themselves.
Can the child correctly compare two groups, one close and the other spread out?	Put four red blocks in a spread-out row, and four blue blocks in a "shoved-together" row. Ask the child whether there are more blue or more red blocks.	Somewhere between five and seven years of age, the child may be able to see that the groups are the same. Until then, the spread-out group will look larger.

FAMILY MATH for Young Children

155

A Question	Something to Try	Things to Look For
Can the child put several objects in order, from smallest to largest, or from largest to smallest?	Put out several objects, not in a row. Ask the child to put them in order, from smallest to largest.	Before age six, most children will not be able to put more than two or three objects in order. If they can't do three objects, go back and try two objects. If they can't do two, wait until later.
Can the child name and describe familiar objects by feel?	Put an object inside a paper bag or box, and have the child reach in and try to describe it, or tell you what it is. Later on, try the same activity with some shapes cut from cardboard. Have some with holes, and some that are familiar, as well as some that are uncommon.	Under age four, children might be able to name a familiar object, such as a comb or cup. They may not be able to give very good descriptions. Don't expect much success before age six or seven. Practice asking questions about things they are playing with, such as "Is it hard or soft?", "Is it warm or cold?", "Is it heavy or light?"

A Question	Something to Try	Things to Look For
Can the child make a straight line with objects?	Put out five or six things that won't roll, such as bottle-caps or blocks. Ask the child to put them in a straight line, from one side of the paper or table to the other.	Under the age of six or seven, the straight line will probably be wavy, even if they use the edge of the table or paper as a guide.
Can the child draw a straight line?	Give the child pencil or crayon and paper, and ask him or her to draw a straight line.	This is about coordination. Accept whatever the child draws. You can't teach coordination. If the child is not able to do this, do more large muscle activity, until much later.

Try not to rush a child's learning. Children's play is truly their work and should be respected as such. Remember, the JOY of learning is the greatest gift for their future.

Are games optional? No, they're a foundation for other learning. As Mary Baratta-Lorton called them, they're "Workjobs."

Sharing FAMILY MATH for Young Children

Sharing FAMILY MATH

Now that you have tried some activities, you know how easy it is to explore mathematical ideas with your child. There are lots of other folks who would love to get together and share their ideas for learning and exploring mathematics.

If you belong to a parents' club, a church group, or volunteer in your child's school, you can share these activities with other families.

This section is designed to help you organize and lead *FAMILY MATH for Young Children* events just about anywhere you can gather people together. When you do, you will join thousands of families through-out the United States and all over the world, who get together for the purpose of sharing mathematical ideas.

This schedule has been tried with families in schools and community centers. You can create a schedule that works best for you. You do not need a lot of fancy materials, but you do need some space for folks to sit and move around.

We recommend that you meet with your group on a regular basis. This allows families to build a community, to gain a deeper understanding of the role mathematics plays in their children's education, and to try out a variety of ways to learn and communicate with their children. Some families meet once a week for an hour and a half, others on the second Tuesday of every month. Meeting with smaller groups allows more people to talk with one another and more ideas to be heard.

Class Evaluation

There are several ways you can evaluate the accomplishments of your FAMILY MATH gatherings. You can find out what went well, what parents liked and want more of, what kids liked, as well as what to plan for in future classes.

Why do an evaluation?

- For my own information, to make improvements for future classes
- For community interest
- For potential supporters, who like to know what they are supporting

Information for improving the FAMILY MATH class

- What do you hope to accomplish?
- Are the directions or instructions clear?
- Are the activities engaging and challenging?
- Are there opportunities for families to infuse their own culture to the concepts or activities?
- Is the class presented in the families' primary language?

Outcomes For Families

- How do you feel about mathematics when attending a FAMILY MATH class?
- How do you feel about it afterwards?
- Who comes? Why did they come? Who did not come? Why not?
- Who did not return after a class? Why not?
- Is your family enjoying math more as a result of attending?
- Will you try some of the activities at home?
- What strategies have you acquired for communicating with your child about mathematics?
- Are you more involved with the school as a result of participating in FAMILY MATH?

- Do you feel more confident in helping your child with mathematics?

SOME EXAMPLES OF EVALUATIONS

Informal comments

Ask parents informally at the beginning of a class:

- Why did you come to FAMILY MATH?

- How did you hear about us?

- What do you hope we will talk about or do today?

Math journals

- Give each family a FAMILY MATH "menu" of a class schedule and planned activities. Ask them to write reflections of their experiences. Children can participate in these evaluations by writing or illustrating, and by having conversations with their parents. Families can keep these to record their own progress, to keep track of the interest centers they visited, or to write questions for the group to address. Ask them to share their journals with you (but do not require it).

Checklists

- Create a checklist. List the activities by name, and ask families to rate them. You can include comments like "Tried it and liked it a lot", "Don't remember that one", "Plan to try it at home", "Didn't like it", "Learned something new", and so on.

Don't forget:

- Keep information confidential.

- Gather only the information you plan to use.

- Listen carefully to suggestions.

- Above all, enjoy yourself!

Planning Check-Sheet

Things to do before FAMILY MATH classes:

WHEN	WHAT
2 months before class	Δ Decide on time and place Δ Decide on grade levels Δ Make arrangements with principal, district office, custodian, or other persons who are involved
About 6 weeks before class	Δ Begin recruiting (Much earlier than 8 weeks and people may forget, and later than 3 weeks doesn't leave enough time for parents to plan)
1 or 2 weeks before each class	Δ Finalize class curriculum Δ Begin to gather needed materials Δ Prepare masters for handouts Δ Line up child care if appropriate
About 2 weeks before the role model panel	Δ Select date and line up role models for career seminar
1 week before class	Δ Run off handouts for week 1 (guess on enrollment) Δ Double-check room availability Δ Send home reminder notices to those signed up
1 day to 2 hours before class	Δ Triple-check room arrangements Δ Set up openers, sign-in sheet Δ Arrange furniture the way you like it Δ Make arrangements for coffee, tea, etc.
When class begins	Δ Relax, it's going to be wonderful!

FAMILY MATH for Young Children

Join us for an evening of family learning

Place:

Time:

Date:

Learn

   △   How to help your child be successful in math

   △   What kind of mathematics your child will be expected to learn in school this year

   △   How to make mathematics more understandable and FUN!

Enjoy

   △   Math activities designed especially for families

   △   Talking with your child about important ideas

   △   Sharing and learning with other families in a positive and friendly environment

Take Home

   △   Games and activities

   △   Information and materials

For more information call:

_____ *Please return to:* _____ *by:* _____

☐ YES, I am interested in having fun with my child at a FAMILY MATH for Young Children class.

Name _____

Address _____

Phone _____

Child's Name _____

Child's Grade _____

Child's Teacher _____

☐ I cannot attend a FAMILY MATH class, but please keep me on your mailing list.

FAMILY MATH Class Notes

SETTING UP

Be sure you have all the necessary material on hand. Have a schedule with the details of the evening and keep a checklist of the materials you will use. Make sure that handouts, activity packages, or other goodies are ready.

Give yourself plenty of time before the class. Some folks will arrive early and you will want to be free to welcome them without the distraction of last-minute details. Have refreshments available.

If you want people to sign in, you can do this in several ways. Besides having a sign-in sheet, you can create a birthday chart, a Venn diagram, a pictogram, or any other way you can think of to collect and organize information.

WELCOME

Create a joyful atmosphere. Be warm, nurturing, and enthusiastic. Welcome families as they arrive. Establishing a comfortable atmosphere will give families the confidence to try out new things, make mistakes, and take some risks.

Your actions should convey the message that math can be fun, that parents are their children's most important teachers, and that we all can learn mathematics. When families concentrate on having fun with math rather than focusing on right answers, your class will be a success.

LET'S BEGIN

It is important to have some centers open when families arrive. Since not everyone will get there at the same time, the centers will give folks an opportunity to get into mathematics the minute they walk in the door. Examples of what these centers might look like are in this chapter.

About ten or fifteen minutes after the official starting time, you can gather everyone together for introductions. Parents can say their name and introduce their children. If the group is large you can do smaller group introductions.

At your first meeting you will want to explain the FAMILY MATH program. Do this in a brief and engaging manner. Young children will not sit still for a long talk session.

ACTIVITIES

You are now ready to begin the first activity. All activities should engage parents and children. You might try role playing with a partner to model different kinds of interactions between parents and children. You can start with any activity in the book — they are not in any hierarchical order. Some will seem similar; this is intentional. Visiting a concept or idea through various activities helps us learn and gain deeper mathematical understanding.

Introduce the activities with clear directions. Talk about the mathematics, make connections to the work world, everyday life, or to the school curriculum. Check for understanding by stopping and asking what strategies folks are using, what patterns they see, or what predictions they want to make. Stress the importance of process, communication, and using available tools. Let families know that simply getting the right answer is not the goal.

Interest Centers

Interest centers allow people to investigate mathematics. Families may set their own pace as they try out problem-solving skills. Your role during this time may be to circulate and talk with them about their ideas and strategies, provide encouragement or suggestions as needed, or try out the centers yourself.

Ask families about their experiences at the centers, and talk about the mathematics. Let them know that it is O.K. if they did not get to all of them. Have the same centers available the next time you get together, and add one or two new ones.

Movement

Allow some time at each gathering for children to get up and move. This is a good time for one class leader to take the children to another room or outdoors for activities such as *I'm A Shape*. Don't forget that children need to use big and little muscles. When the children return to the room, they can teach their parents the new ways they learned to move.

Parent Talk.

While the children are trying out the movement activities, adults stay with a class facilitator or leader to share strategies for working with their children. Parents may have questions about mathematics reform, or other topics of interest. You do not have to be experts to address the issues at hand. If you need further resources for future discussions, the group can generate a list of available resources, or invite guests to provide more information. In one class, parents shared ideas about types of questions to ask their children, in another parents asked questions about the changes in mathematics books. Whatever the topic, be sure to give everyone a chance to be heard.

TAKE-HOME MATERIALS

Be sure to have materials and extra copies of the activities for families to try out at home. At your next class meeting discuss the activities. Ask questions about the mathematics, new discoveries, or interesting experiences with the activities.

CLOSURE

Be sure to have time at the end of the session for farewells. Let everyone know that you look forward to seeing them next time and don't forget to thank the children for bringing their parents. Also, you might mention what special topics the group will be investigating next time.

Have fun!

FAMILY MATH for Young Children
Sample Schedule
Day 1

TIME	WHO	ACTIVITY AND NOTES	MATERIALS
6:00		**Interest Centers** • Rag Bag • Directions: All in a Row • Directions: Color Lines of Three • Many Shapes • Estimation Jar	• 1" blocks • crayons • 1" grid paper • pieces of various types of fabrics • paste • 3"x 3" squares (index cards for Rag Bag) • lids (for tracing) • scratch paper • various shapes • 2 estimation jars: one with more than 10 but less than 20 items, one with less than 10 items
6:15		**Welcome** **Introductions** Parents say who they are and introduce their child. **Class Overview**	
6:25		**Paper Plate Math**	• paper plates, scissors
6:40		**Interest Centers**	
7:10		**Parent Talk/Movement** • Parents stay in to discuss the mathematics. • Children go with another person to try the activities.	
7:15		**Movement** • Inside, Outside, On **Parent Talk** • Parents choose topics **FMYC Concepts in Centers:** • estimation • comparing • logic • patterns • organizing information	For Movement: sidewalk chalk For Parent Talk: FM handout/cartoon
7:25		**Farewells**	
7:30		**Session ends**	

FAMILY MATH for Young Children
Sample Schedule
Day 2

TIME	WHO	ACTIVITY AND NOTES	MATERIALS
6:00		**Interest Centers** • Estimation Corner • Scales • Rag Bag • Seashells • Tell Me What You See • This is In and This is Not • Estimation Jar	• scale • counters or cubes • blocks • fabric, index cards • scissors • seashells • rocks, plants, shells, other materials to compare and talk about • Estimation Jar
6:15		**Welcome** **Introductions** • Children introduce parents. **Overview**	
6:25		**Me and My Toys** • Comparing heights	• toys • adding machine tape • pencils and crayons • tape
6:40		**Interest Centers** see above	
7:10		**Movement** **Rhythm Patterns** **Parent Talk** **Parents choose the topics** • Mathematics and play • What should I be looking for? • What does my child understand about math? • Teaching by doing, being lifelong learners	• ourselves • handout: "How's My Child Doing?"
7:25		**Farewells**	
7:30		**Take Home Activities: Rag Bag** **FMYC session ends**	

FAMILY MATH for Young Children
Sample Schedule
Day 3

Time	Who	Activity and Notes	Materials
6:00		**Refreshments** **Interest Centers** • Estimation Corner • Scales • Many Shapes • This is In and This is Not • Aquariums • Make-a-Pair • Color Lines of Three	• scale • counters • toys, yarn • goldfish crackers • concentration cards • color cubes
6:15		**Welcome** **Introductions** • Kids: Tell one thing fun or interesting you enjoy doing with your family. **Overview**	
6:25		**Many Shapes** **Venn Diagrams** • Shoes With Laces • Wearing Glasses • Wearing Red/Blue	• yarn
6:40		**Interest Centers**	
7:10		**Movement** • Now I Am Tall **Parent Talk** **Parents choose the topic** • Parent Issues • Expectations • Math in Kindergarten • Portfolios • FMYC at Your Child's School	• FM Folder with activities for older children
7:25		Farewells	
7:30		**Take Home Activities: Make-a-Pair** **FMYC session ends**	

FAMILY MATH for Young Children
Sample Schedule
Day 4

TIME	WHO	ACTIVITY AND NOTES	MATERIALS
6:00		**Interest Centers** • Make-a-Pair • Color Lines of Four • Scales • Many Shapes • Estimation Jars • Aquariums	• cards with pictures • blocks • scales • bag of various small items • crayons • chart paper • goldfish crackers
6:15		**Welcome** **Introductions** • Which interest center will you visit today? **Class Overview**	
6:25		**Measurement** • Measuring feet • Hands • Height	• pencils • butcher paper • adding machine tape • yarn or string
6:40		**Centers** see above	
7:10		**Movement** **Shadows** **Parent Talk** **Parents choose the topics** • Kindergarten • Curriculum • Other Math Resources • Manipulatives • Rote Learning	• outdooors
7:25		**Farewells**	
7:30		**Take-Home Activity: Look for Shadows** **FMYC session ends**	

FAMILY MATH for Young Children
Sample Planning Sheet

TIME	WHO	ACTIVITY AND NOTES	MATERIALS

Interest Centers and Samples

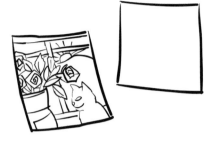

Interest centers are areas where families can explore math ideas independently. They provide lots of fun and engaging ways to investigate and try out mathematical ideas.

No matter what time you plan to start, families will arrive at different times. Interest centers are an excellent way to get folks engaged in mathematics from the moment they arrive.

Many of the games and activities in this book can be set up as interest centers. The following pages are just a few examples of how activities can be adapted to more independent investigations and explorations. Keep in mind that these are just models. You can let your imagination soar, and create colorful, large posters.

You might want to post some sample questions near the centers, so parents can keep the "math talk" going while working with their child. There are examples of these types of questions in the *Questions That Promote Mathematical Thinking* section.

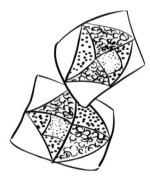

Families don't have to visit *all* the stations in one evening. Let them know that the centers will be there the next time they come. Provide a list of the centers, so families can mark the ones they have done. This way, families won't worry that they don't get to visit all of them.

We have provided a sample of what a list might look like. You can design your own if you like. You might also want to provide a space where families can evaluate or assess their experiences. They can show which activities they enjoyed, something they learned, or anything they want to include.

MITTENS AND GLOVES

Use a crayon to trace your hand with your thumb and fingers spread apart.

Guess (estimate) how many squares will cover your hand.

Cover your shape with the squares and count how many it takes to cover it.

What was the difference between your guess and how many it actually took to cover your hand? How did you figure out the difference?

MITTENS AND GLOVES

Trace your other hand with your fingers together, and your thumb out.

Guess (estimate) how many squares will cover the shape of your hand.

Cover the hand shape with squares. How many did it take to cover your hand's shape?

Could you use something else to cover the shapes? Try it, and count again!

ARM SPAN

Just for fun, measure the distance from the tip of the longest finger on one hand to the tip of the longest finger on your other hand. Ask someone to help you measure!

Cut this piece of yarn and connect your glove and mitten together with it.

Use this to measure objects in the room like a chair, a door, and stuff like that.

What other things can you find that are as wide (or as tall) as your arm span? Make a list.

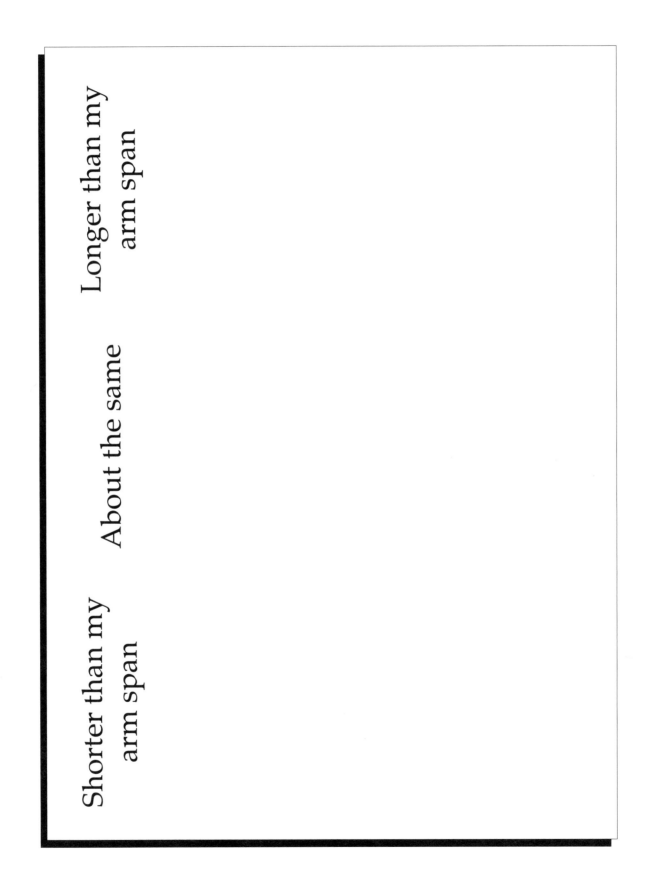

Longer than my
arm span

About the same

Shorter than my
arm span

LEAF TREASURES

Pick a leaf from the pile (one for each of you).

Compare your leaves.

Count with your partner how many pointed ends your leaf has.

How are they the same?

How are they different?

How many squares do you think your leaf will cover?

Trace your leaf on the graph paper. Count the squares your leaf covered.

More Resources

Mathematics Generally Covered

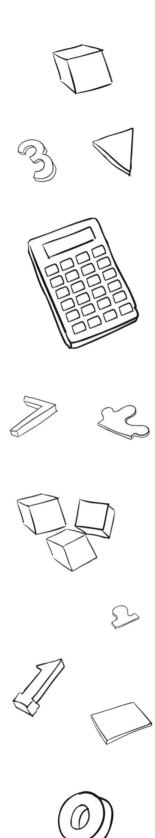

The following pages list the mathematics generally covered in the grade levels from kindergarten through eighth grade.

Your own school or district will have its own list of skills for each grade level, which may look somewhat different. There is no hard and fast rule about the age at which students should learn most topics, and lists such as these should be considered general guidelines rather than absolute musts.

We have tried to emphasize the development of topics we feel are most important, and for that reason have placed application of mathematics in the context of daily living at the top of the list. Estimation is also mentioned repeatedly throughout, since it can give students power in applying mathematics.

We also believe that children should be allowed to use calculators in the same way adults would — to take the drudgery out of long and tedious calculations. This requires that children be taught how to use calculators with the same seriousness with which they are taught arithmetic skills. It also suggests, for example, that once the long division algorithm is understood, there is no benefit from doing page after page of long division problems. The time is better spent on using new word problem solution strategies, learning how to make another kind of graph, finding patterns in mathematics tables, or any of thousands of other fascinating activities.

It is extremely important that children be allowed to proceed at their own pace and not be forced to conform to this or any other list. If the list says, for example, that students should be able to count by twos, threes, fours, fives, and tens, but your child is really struggling with counting by ones, please do not press him or her to do more. Use lists with caution!

182

Preschool – Age Four

This list represents some things your child would experience in a preschool class. Many of these occur naturally as your child develops.

Applications

Δ   Exploring mathematics concepts in everyday events

Δ   Talking with others about math experiences

Classifying

Δ   Describing items by similarities and differences

Δ   Comparing by describing characteristics of two objects

Geometry

Δ   Distinguishing and describing shapes, circles, triangles, squares, and rectangles

Δ   Drawing or tracing shapes with some accuracy

Numbers

Δ   Arranging sets of objects in one-to-one correspondence

Δ   Comparing number of objects in various groupings

Δ   Making connections between objects and numbers in groups

Δ   Counting objects

Measurement

Δ   Comparing weights/lengths/heights of different objects

Δ   Employing non-standard units of measure

Developing Spatial Sense

Δ   Investigating order: next to, in between, first/last

Δ   Recognizing proximity: near/far, above/below

KINDERGARTEN

Applications

Δ   Talking about mathematics used in our daily lives

Δ   Exploring mathematics in everyday events

Numbers

Δ   Learning to estimate how many

Δ   Counting objects, up to about 15 or 20

Δ   Putting out objects to match a number

Δ   Comparing two sets of objects

Δ   Recognizing numerals up to 20

Δ   Writing numerals, 0 through 9

Δ   Learning about ordinal numbers, such as first, second, third

Measurement

Δ   Estimating and comparing:
    Taller or shorter, longer or wider
    Largest or smallest, heavier or lighter

Geometry

Δ   Recognizing and classifying colors and simple shapes

Δ   Holding more than one attribute in mind at a time

Patterns

Δ   Recognizing simple patterns, continuing them, and making up new patterns

Probability and Statistics

Δ   Making and talking about simple graphs of everyday things, such as birthdays, pets, food, and so on

First Grade

Applications

Δ   Talking about mathematics used in daily living

Δ   Learning strategies such as using manipulatives or drawing diagrams to solve problems

Arithmetic and Numbers

Δ   Practicing estimation skills

Δ   Counting through about 100

Δ   Recognizing, writing, and being able to order numbers through about 100

Δ   Counting by twos, fives, and tens

Δ   Using ordinal numbers, such as first, second, tenth, and so on

Δ   Learning basic addition and subtraction facts up to 9+9=18 and 18-9=9

Δ   Developing understanding of place value using tens and ones with manipulatives, including base ten blocks, Cuisenaire rods, abaci, play money, and so on

Δ   Developing the concept of fractional values such as halves, thirds, and fourths

Measurement

Δ   Telling time to the hour or half-hour (but don't press if not mastered)

Δ   Recognizing and using calendars, days of the week, months

Δ   Estimating lengths and measuring things with non-standard units, such as how many handprints across the table

Δ   Understanding uses and relative values of pennies, nickels, dimes

Geometry and Patterns

Δ   Working with shapes, such as triangles, circles, squares, rectangles

Δ   Recognizing, repeating, and making up geometric and numeric patterns

Probability and Statistics

Δ   Making and interpreting simple graphs, of everyday things, such as color preferences, favorite snacks, number of brothers and sisters, and so on

Second Grade

Applications

Δ   Talking about mathematics used in daily life

Δ   Creating and solving word problems in measurement, geometry, probability, and statistics, as well as arithmetic

Δ   Practicing strategies for solving problems, such as drawing diagrams, organized guessing, putting problems into own words, and so on

Numbers

Δ   Practicing estimation skills

Δ   Reading and writing numbers through about 1,000, playing around with up to 10,000

Δ   Counting by twos, fives, and tens, and maybe some other numbers for fun

Δ   Learning about odd and even numbers

Δ   Using ordinal numbers such as first, second, tenth

Δ   Identifying fractions such as halves, thirds, quarters

Δ   Understanding and using the signs for greater than (>) and less than (<)

Arithmetic

Δ   Knowing addition and subtraction facts through 9+9=18 and 18-9=9

Δ   Estimating answers to other addition and subtraction problems

Δ   Practicing addition and subtraction with and without regrouping (carrying)

Δ   Adding columns of numbers

Δ   Exploring uses of a calculator

Δ   Being introduced to multiplication and division

Geometry

Δ   Finding congruent shapes (same size and shape)

Δ   Recognizing and naming squares, rectangles, circles, and maybe some other polygons

Δ   Informally recognizing lines of symmetry

Δ   Reading and drawing very simple maps

Measurement

Δ   Practicing estimation of measurements – how many toothpicks long is the table?

Δ   Comparing lengths, areas, weights

Δ   Measuring with non-standard units, beginning to use some standard units such as inches or centimeters

Δ   Telling time to the nearest quarter-hour, maybe to the minute

Δ   Making change with coins and bills, doing money problems with manipulatives

Δ   Knowing days of the week and months, and using the calendar to find dates

Probability and Statistics

Δ   Making and interpreting simple graphs, using physical objects or manipulatives

Δ   Doing simple probability activities

Patterns

Δ   Working with patterns of numbers, shapes, colors, sounds, and so on, including adding to existing patterns, completing missing sections, making up new patterns

THIRD GRADE

Applications

Δ   Talking about mathematics seen in students' lives

Δ   Creating, analyzing, and solving word problems in all of the concept areas

Δ   Practicing a variety of problem-solving strategies with problems of more than one step

Numbers

Δ   Practicing estimation skills with all problems

Δ   Reading and writing numbers through about 10,000, exploring those beyond 10,000

Δ   Counting by twos, threes, fours, fives and tens and other numbers

Δ   Naming and comparing fractions, such as 1/2 is greater than 1/4

Δ   Identifying fractions of a whole number, such as 1/2 of 12 is 6

Δ   Exploring concepts of decimal numbers, such as tenths and hundredths, using money to represent values

Δ   Using the signs for greater than (>) and less than (<)

Arithmetic

Δ   Learning how to use calculators effectively

Δ   Using calculators to solve problems

Δ   Continuing to practice basic addition and subtraction facts and simple addition and subtraction problems

Δ   Doing larger and more complicated addition and subtraction problems

Δ   Beginning to learn multiplication and division facts through 9x9=81 and 81÷9=9

Δ   Beginning to learn multiplication and division of two-and three-digit numbers by a single-digit number

Δ   Learning about remainders

Geometry

Δ   Recognizing and naming shapes such as squares, rectangles, trapezoids, triangles, circles, and three-dimensional objects such as cubes, cylinders, and the like

Δ   Identifying congruent shapes (same size and shape)

Δ   Recognizing lines of symmetry, and reflections (mirror images) and translations (movements to a different position) of figures

Δ   Reading and drawing simple maps, using coordinates

Δ   Learning about parallel (| |) and perpendicular (⊥) lines

Measurement

Δ   Estimating before doing measurement

Δ   Using non-standard and some standard units to measure:
    ◊   Length
        (toothpicks, straws, paper strips, string lengths, and so on)
        centimeters, decimeters, meters, inches, feet, yards)
    ◊   Perimeters
        (same as length)
    ◊   Area
        (square units)
        (paper squares, tiles, and so on)
        (square centimeters, meters, inches, feet, yards)
    ◊   Weight
        (paper clips, rocks, blocks, beans, and so on)
        (grams, kilograms, ounces, pounds)
    ◊   Volume and capacity
        (blocks, rice, beans, water; in cans, paper cups, and so on)
        (liters, cubic centimeters, cups, gallons, pints, quarts)
    ◊   Temperature
        (°Celsius, °Fahrenheit)

Δ   Telling time, probably to the nearest minute

Δ   Continuing to use money to develop understanding of decimals

Δ   Using calendars

Probability and Statistics

Δ   Being introduced to probability concepts, such as the chance of something happening

Δ   Using tally marks, collecting and organizing informal data

Δ   Making, reading, and interpreting simple graphs

Patterns

Δ   Continuing to work with patterns, including those found on addition and multiplication charts

Resources

Look for these at your library or local bookstore, or contact the publishers listed.

Allison, Linda and Martha Weston. *Eenie Meenie Miney Math! Math Play for You and Your Preschooler*. Boston, Massachusetts: Little, Brown, and Company, 1993.

Apelman, Maja and Julie King. *Exploring Everyday Math: Ideas for Students, Teachers, and Parents*. Portsmouth, New Hampshire: Heinemann, 1993.

Baratta-Lorton, Mary. *Mathematics Their Way*. Menlo Park, California: Addison-Wesley Publishing Co., 1976.

Baratta-Lorton, Mary. *Workjobs… For Parents*. Menlo Park, California: Addison-Wesley Publishing Co., 1972.

Harnadek, Anita. *Mindbenders Levels A, B, C*. Pacific Grove, California: Midwest Publications, 1978.

Kaye, Peggy. *Games for Math: Playful Ways to Help Your Child Learn Math, From Kindergarten to Third Grade*. New York, New York: Pantheon Books, 1987.

Kelly, Marguerite and Elia Parsons. *The Mother's Almanac, Revised*. New York, New York: Main Street Books, Doubleday, 1992.

Richards, Roy and Lesley Jones. *An Early Start to Mathematics*. London, United Kingdom: MacDonald & Co.

Schreiner, Bryson. *Arithmetic Games and Aids for Early Childhood*. Hayward, California: Activity Resources Company, Inc., 1974.

Wirtz, Robert. *Making Friends with Numbers, Kits I and II*. Monterey, California: Curriculum Development Associates, 1977.

Zaslavsky, Claudia. *Preparing Young Children for Math: A Book of Games*. New York, New York: Schocken Books, 1979.

GEMS (Great Explorations in Math and Science) Program, Lawrence Hall of Science, University of California, Berkeley, California 94720-5200.

PEACHES, Lawrence Hall of Science, University of California, Berkeley, California 94720-5200.

Bibliography

Atkinson, Sue, ed. *Mathematics with Reason: The Emergent Approach to Primary Maths*. Portsmouth, New Hampshire: Heinemann, 1992.

Bredekamp, Sue and Teresa Rosegrant. *Reaching Potentials: Appropriate Curriculum and Assessment for Young Children, Vol. 1*. Washington, District of Columbia: National Association for the Education of Young Children, 1992.

Bredekamp, Sue, ed. *Developmentally Appropriate Practice in Early Childhood Programs Serving Children From Birth Through Age 8*. Washington, District of Columbia: National Association for the Education of Young Children, 1987.

Child Development Project. *At Home in Our Schools*. Oakland, California: Child Development Project, 1994.

Downie, Diane, Twila Slesnick, and Jean K. Stenmark. *Math for Girls and Other Problem Solvers*. Berkeley, California: Lawrence Hall of Science, University of California, 1981.

FAMILY MATH. *We All Count in FAMILY MATH*. Berkeley, California: FAMILY MATH (Matemática Para La Familia) EQUALS, Lawrence Hall of Science, University of California. Videocassette.

Kamii, Constance and Rheta DeVries. *Group Games in Early Education: Implications of Piaget's Theory*. Washington, District of Columbia: National Association for the Education of Young Children, 1980.

Meiring, Stephen P. *Parents and the Teaching of Mathematics*. Columbus, Ohio: Ohio Department of Education, 1980.

National Association for the Education of Young Children. *Good Teaching Practices for Older Preschoolers and Kindergartners*. Washington, District of Columbia: National Association for the Education of Young Children.

Sprung, Barbara, Patricia B. Campbell, and Merle Froschl. *What Will Happen if... Young Children and the Scientific Method*. New York, New York: Education Equity Concepts, Inc., 1985.

Index

A

Acknowledging Your Child's Work, 24
Activity Pages Include, 28

B

bibliography, 193
Button Boxes, 62
Button, Button, Where Is The Button?, 66

C

Camp, Ernestine, 74
Carlyle, Ann, 74
change over time, 135
children
    communication with, 17, 22, 24, 97
    working with, 30
Class Evaluation, 161
Collections, 140
Copy-Cats, 42
Create a Puzzle Jr., 52

D

Direction, 54
    All In a Row, 58
    Color Lines of Four, 61
    Color Lines of Three, 60
    Which Direction?, 56
drawing, 147

E

evaluations
    checklists, 162
    math journals, 162
Everyday Estimation, 20

F

FAMILY MATH
    class
        activities, 166
        interest center examples, 175
        interest centers, 167, 174
        movement, 167
        parents, 167
        sample planning sheet, 173
        sample schedule, 169
        take-home materials, 168
    class notes, 165
    sample invitation, 164

H

homework, 17–18
How's My Child Doing?, 152

I

I Remember When I Was Young, xi
I'm A Shape, 84
Inside, Outside, On, 40

L

language, 50, 66, 144
    description, 97, 114, 120
    recognition of letters, 105
Leaf Treasures, 144
Linehan, Anne, 70
Looking at Letters, 105
Love Notes Quilt Patch, 94

M

Make a Game, 128
Make-a-Pair, 100
    Hidden Matches, 102
    Match for Five, 102
    Mini-Pairs, 101
    Pairs, 101
Make-a-Pair Cards, 103
Making Spinners, 132
Many Shapes, 92
mathematics
    adding, 62, 142
    addition, 100
    area, 145
    bar chart, 34
    counting, 37, 68, 124, 126
    design, 73
    estimating, 68, 144
    geometry, 50, 52, 73, 92, 94, 97
    language in, 46
    learning, 16–17
    logic, 66, 70, 74
        sorting, 126
    misc. charts, 35, 36
    number, 146, 148
    numbers, 62, 74, 128
    ordinal numbers, 66
    patterns, 73, 88, 94, 98
    pre-algebra, 74
    probability, 128
    puzzles, 52
    quantity, 148

M (continued)

mathematics (continued)
  recognition of numerals, 105
  sets, 90, 146, 148
  shapes, 38, 40
  size, 38, 46
  sorting, 90
  spatial reasoning, 42
  symmetry, 42, 44
  Venn diagram, 32
  visual reasoning, 37
Mathematics Generally Covered, 182
  first grade, 185
  kindergarten, 184
  pre-school, 183
  second grade, 187
  third grade, 189
Mathematics In Your Home, 16
Me and My Toys, 118
Measuring Spoons, 68
memories, xi, 100
memory, 124
Mixtures - Bean Salads and Fish Bowls, 74
Moon and Stars, 88
muscle development
  big muscles, 84
  small muscles, 73
My Rule, Your Rule, 126

N

Name That Shape, 97
Now I Am Tall, 38
Nuts and Bolts, 37

O

observing, 105, 114, 116, 120
observing change, 88
Organizing Information, 30

P

Papel Picado, 44
Paper Plate Math, 70
  Three-Color Questions, 72
  Two-Color Questions, 72
Patterns All Around, 98
planning, 128
Planning Check Sheet, 163

Q

Questions That Promote
    Mathematical Thinking, 22

R

Rag Bag, 46
reasoning, 70
resources, 192
Return to Earth! game, 128
Rocks, 148

S

Same Yet Different, 90
Seashells, 146
Shadows, 135
Share a Square Mobile, 50
Sharing FAMILY MATH, 160
Smith, Carol, 70
sorting, 142
spatial relations, 84
  direction, 54
  length, 118
  measurement, 68, 135
  reasoning, 94
  space, 118
Stamps Galore!, 142

T

Tell Me What You See, 114
testing, 18
texture, 46
This is In and This is Not, 120
time, 135
Tracing Shapes, 73

W

What is FAMILY MATH?, xii
What is Missing?, 124
What's Alike About You and Me?, 116